WITHDRAWN

CROSSING THE LINE

A FEARLESS TEAM *of* BROTHERS *and the* SPORT THAT CHANGED THEIR LIVES FOREVER

KAREEM ROSSER

ST. MARTIN'S PRESS
NEW YORK

First published in the United States by St. Martin's Press,
an imprint of St. Martin's Publishing Group

www.stmartins.com

Designed by Devan Norman

Library of Congress Cataloging-in-Publication Data

Names: Rosser, Kareem, author.
Title: Crossing the line : a fearless team of brothers and the sport
    that changed their lives forever / Kareem Rosser.
Description: First edition. | New York : St. Martin's Press, 2021.
Identifiers: LCCN 2020037478 | ISBN 9781250270863
    (hardcover) | ISBN 9781250270870 (ebook)
Subjects: LCSH: Rosser, Kareem. | African American polo
    players—Biography. | Polo players—United States—Biography. |
    Brothers—Pennsylvania—Philadelphia—Biography. |
    Philadelphia (Pa.)—Biography.
Classification: LCC GV1010.32.R67 A3 2021 | DDC
    796.35/3092 [B]—dc23
LC record available at https://lccn.loc.gov/2020037478

Our books may be purchased in bulk for promotional, educational,
or business use. Please contact your local bookseller or the
Macmillan Corporate and Premium Sales Department at
1-800-221-7945, extension 5442, or by email at
MacmillanSpecialMarkets@macmillan.com.

First Edition: 2021

10 9 8 7 6 5 4 3 2 1

CROSSING THE LINE

DISCLAIMER

This is a work of creative nonfiction. The stories in this book are based on my experience and real-life events, although some names and identifying details have been changed, and some events have been compressed or adjusted in deference to the larger story. Conversations in the book are not recounted verbatim but rather are meant to evoke the meaning and feeling of what was said.

A NOTE TO THE READER

I have been explaining the rules of polo to curious strangers and friends since I was nine years old. I wrote this story with the intention that you should be able to absorb the rules of the game chapter by chapter as you read through, but if you would like a brief tutorial on polo ahead of the story, please skip forward to the appendix entitled "The Rules of Polo" at the end of this book.

Started from the bottom,
now we're here.
Started from the bottom,
now my whole team fuckin' here.

—DRAKE

CROSSING THE LINE

PROLOGUE

F oul! Dangerous riding!" the ref shouted across the arena.
The crowd roared back in response—a few in support of his call, but most of them groaning in anger. We were at the very end of the fourth chukker, one point behind, and I'd just been given the chance to make a two-point goal.

Steam rose off the body of my pony and left a misty trail behind me as I galloped back onto the field. I smiled to myself and just barely resisted pumping my fist in excitement.

I should have been pissed. The captain of the other team, a big blond dude with the kind of deep tan that only comes from spending Christmas in Aruba, had just illegally boarded me, coming out of nowhere and riding up so close and fast that he had slammed me and my pony into the wooden wall surrounding the arena. He'd thrown me a nasty sneer as he pinned me to the wood, and then galloped off, hit-and-run style, hoping the ref wouldn't notice. He was playing rough, breaking rules, and he could have easily hurt both me and my horse. In fact, my shoulder was throbbing from the blow and I knew I'd feel it for days. But I shook it off and grinned. I couldn't be angry. Because if he was playing rough, that meant we were finally being taken seriously as a team. If he was playing rough, it meant that he actually thought we could win.

—

THREE YEARS EARLIER

It was always our boots that gave us away.

I mean, it didn't exactly help that we showed up to the polo club, one of the top facilities in the country, in our coach Lezlie's old junker of a car, the one that smelled like fast food and road-trip stink and was missing a hubcap. My two teammates and I crammed into our seats between all the gear, desperate as hell to get out after being forced to listen to two hundred fifty miles of *All Things Considered*.

I'm also sure it did not go unnoticed that one of my Work to Ride teammates, my little brother Gerb, was still so small that he had to use both hands to lift his polo mallet, and the other one, Drea, was mean-mugging like he'd kick your ass if you even looked at him wrong.

Because these were the only riders available for us to play against, we were scheduled to match up with a team of full-grown, eighteen-year-old, high-school seniors from a top-seeded military academy. So it was also pretty noticeable that we had barely hit puberty. I was the oldest at fifteen, and Gerb and Drea were both thirteen.

It was definitely more than obvious that we were the only Black faces within a one-hundred-acre radius of the arena.

But what really gave up our game was just south of our knees. They might look past our age and race and Lezlie's crappy car, but as soon as they saw our hand-me-down, duct-taped, ill-sized, janky old fake-leather boots, they all knew that we were in the wrong place. Those boots made it instantly clear that my teammates and I did not belong in the exclusive, expensive world of polo.

We stood for a moment, stretching and rubbing our eyes. Back at home in Philly, it was still icy, gray, and freezing, but here in Virginia the air was sweet and mild, the sky was brilliant blue, and the seventy-five acres of rolling hills that surrounded us on all sides were covered in the softest, greenest grass we had seen for months.

From where we stood, we could see the regulation-size, professional-level polo field, the acres of white-fenced corrals and pastures, and the perfectly groomed outdoor practice spaces. We were playing indoors today, in the immense polo arena attached to the stables.

Our team came from The Bottom, a neighborhood in Philadelphia where you had a better chance of being incarcerated or getting shot than graduating from high school. We grew up in a city that had one of the highest murder rates *per capita* in the nation, and that number seemed to be mainly fueled by what went down on a daily basis in our hood.

Our team had almost no funding and a bunch of donated-because-nobody-wanted-them-anymore ponies who were stabled in the middle of Fairmount Park. The barn was leased from the city by Lezlie for a dollar a year, and it showed. No indoor ring, no real fields or regulation riding spaces. She'd built the program bit by bit, scraping to get by. All the barn work was done by volunteers and kids who participated in the program. During the warmer months, we practiced polo across the street in a bumpy soccer field, fighting for space with picnickers and ultimate Frisbee teams in the good weather. Between October and April, when the ground would freeze and the cold and ice made it too dangerous to play in the soccer field, we simply didn't practice at all. In fact, the only time we even had a chance to ride during polo season was when we traveled to play an actual game in an indoor stadium.

We gathered up our stuff and followed Lezlie toward the arena, threading our way through the crowds of polo players, grooms, and coaches, all here, like us, for the Southeast Regional Tournament. I mainly kept my head down, wanting to stay out of the way, but occasionally glancing up to see the other players: young men and women in multicolored jerseys and immaculate white jeans, carrying their gear and leading their shiny, muscled ponies. They came from prep schools and military academies from all over the country, some driving in like we had, but in their own BMWs and Audis, or, in the case of the team we were playing, arriving in a borrowed private jet.

We entered the stables connected to the arena, and immediately, I felt more at ease. All good barns, no matter how fancy or modest, smell the same: a tinge of dust and damp, the warm scent of horse manure and hay, and the sweet, comforting musk of the animals themselves. That smell meant home to me; it made me walk a little easier.

We began to groom the ponies that had been put aside for us—pro-level horses, glowing with health, stamping and snorting, ready to run. They were worlds away from our hand-me-down herd back home. I tried to hide my wonder and envy as I touched the first pony I would ride, running the curry comb over her already gleaming coat, sliding my hands over her sleek, dark neck, strapping on the saddle over her thickly muscled back. I loved our horses back in Philly but I knew that they were junkers compared to this expensive, perfectly trained Ferrari of an animal. For a moment I let myself believe that riding a pony this fine was surely all I would need to win.

"Hey, Kareem, help me out?" asked Gerb, bringing me back down to earth. He needed me to roll the leather on his stirrups because he was so small that even pulling them up to the last hole still left them too long for his little-kid legs. I interlaced my fingers so I could throw him into the saddle, then I jerked the stirrups as I high as I could get them and started to roll, trying to reach the soles of his dangling size-three boots.

As we groomed, I looked around, wondering where the other team was. There was a small crowd of people prepping what I assumed must be their string of ponies, but they were obviously the grooms who had flown over with them, not the players themselves.

It wasn't until we entered the arena, leading our horses behind us, that we finally came face-to-face with our opposing team. It was made up of eight big, strapping white boys—two fresh players for every chukker. They were clean-cut almost-men with rigid military posture and the look of athletes who didn't know how to lose. Lezlie had told us a little about them, so I knew that back at their Midwestern school, they had hundreds of perfectly groomed acres, access to a

string of specially trained, high-goal polo ponies, and one of
the finest indoor arenas in the nation where they could practice every day, year-round, if they wanted to.

Their coach was a lean, good-looking, ex-pro ten-goal
player who was known for his no-mercy approach on the
field. In later years, he would go on to be a private coach
for one of his more talented players, being paid in the high
six figures to fly all over the world with his charge. Our
coach was a frazzled-looking, middle-aged white lady who
spent most of her time just trying to make sure her players
actually made it to and from her barn without getting shot.
Lezlie had left her nine-to-five job with her family's business so she could sink her every last dollar into creating a
barn where kids who had the bleakest of futures could find
a home away from home and a chance to change their lives
for the better.

The opposing players nodded blankly as we filed by.
You would think that maybe the novelty of playing polo
with actual children from the inner city would have made
some kind of impression on them, but the distant looks on
their faces seemed to say that we were nothing but name-
less distractions to trample over on their way to the championship.

I felt a little chill as I looked back over my shoulder. They
were standing there, seemingly unmoved by the noise of
the crowd gathering in the bleachers, the ponies being hot-
walked around the arena, the other waiting horses stamping
and steaming in their pens. They were wearing burgundy
jerseys, white jeans, leather kneepads, and of course, all of
them—every last one these guys—had perfectly broken-in,

gleaming and slick, Fagliano boots, a pair of which were easily worth more than Lezlie's car.

—

Still, I thought, like I always thought—maybe because I
was a fool, or maybe because I just wanted it so goddamned
much—*maybe today will be different. Maybe today, we won't lose.*

—

We were seeded last place but, as always, we went into the
game thinking we had a shot. We jumped onto those borrowed ponies—the nicest mounts we had ever ridden—and
charged into that arena like we were young princes, three
kids full of hope and unearned confidence.

As we rode onto to the field for the coin toss, I glanced
up into the bleachers and saw a sea of white faces: other players and coaches—curious about our game and ducking in to
watch a chukker or two—University of Virginia students
who had a taste for the ponies, local polo fans and paying
members of the club, and then, filling out the crowd, the
parents and families who had flown halfway across the country to cheer on their sons.

Those happy families made me think about the people—*my
people*—who weren't there. My mom and two sisters, Kareema and Washika, back in The Bottom. My two older
brothers, David and Bee, one in prison and one heading that
way. My best friend, Mecca, gone three years now . . . I tried
to push away the ache I felt about the fact that they never
saw us play. We had Lezlie, I reminded myself, who was not
just our coach, but our biggest fan, and we had each other.

That was not nothing. And, I thought, as I always did before a game, I would do my best to play for all of them, even if they couldn't be there to see it. I imagined myself scoring the winning goal, and smiled as I galloped forward, that expertly trained horse flowing like water beneath me, to meet the other team captain for the coin toss.

Even when the odds were so ridiculously stacked against us, as the leader of the team, it was still part of my job to hope. Game after losing game, if we made even one goal, I'd be convinced that we'd finally hit our stride. Two goals and I'd be dreaming about championships, my own stables and the polo dynasty I would leave behind for my grandchildren.

But those dreams had a way of becoming a nightmare awfully quick. We'd only been playing five minutes before the fatal cracks in our team started to show.

It began with Gerb. My little brother was fearless on a horse. Maybe he didn't look like much yet, but he had all the makings of a great player. He ran his pony full tilt, leaned out so far for the ball that he practically swept the ground with his nose, and played defense like the nearly five years and hundred-fifty-pound difference between him and the opposing team was nothing at all. He'd ride along at full speed, his mallet trailing behind him, and when he had a chance to take a swing, he was so small that he'd have to grasp onto his horse with his knees and use both hands to pick up the mallet and make his move. The kid was all heart. But Gerb also had a red-hot, hair-trigger temper. Absolutely anything could set him off, and when he wasn't playing like a mini-pro, he was melting down into violent and uncontrollable tantrums.

Sometimes the teams we played against would realize how green and outmatched we were and hold back a bit, let us score a gentleman's goal or two, or at least not take the opportunity to totally plow us into the ground and stomp our bodies into a pulp. I'm not saying that it was my favorite thing when this happened—nobody loves a pity point—but it did make the game a little easier on our young egos.

These guys were not one of those teams.

The difference was stark. Lezlie babied us before we got onto the field, telling us that, win or lose, she was proud of us either way. That she believed in us. That we were superstars just for showing up. It both embarrassed and pleased us, like having an overly affectionate mother kissing us goodbye in front of our friends as we headed off to school.

Their coach didn't seem to believe in the same kind of positive reinforcement. "Just remember!" he shouted at his boys, "We're here to do nothing but win!"

And apparently his team took these instructions to heart. They wasted no time in hooking our mallets, taking the ball, and leaving us in their dust. They made their first goal, then another one, and then one more after that. It began to feel mean-spirited. They weren't even going to bother to pretend that we were any kind of match for them. It was like we weren't even on the field.

I could see Gerb starting to lose his cool from all the way across the arena. He felt the humiliation keenly and I knew his barely existent impulse control was not going to hold for long.

"Hey," I yelled at him as we both galloped toward the ball, "Chill out, bro!" But Gerb just scowled. He had a look in his eyes that I knew all too well.

I reached the ball first and hooked it right out from under the other team captain and sent it flying. My heart leaped with hope. "Lean out, Drea!" I shouted as the ball came hurtling toward him. He had an open path to our goal.

But Drea did what Drea always did—he stayed in his saddle and let the ball go right past him. He didn't even try to get in there and mix it up.

"C'mon, man!" I yelled.

"We're in the hole," he yelled back. "I'm not getting killed for a game we're just gonna lose!"

Off his horse, Drea was one of the toughest, meanest kids I knew. He basically spent all his daytime hours walking around looking for a fight. He'd use any excuse to take down anybody for just about anything. He was always showing up to the barn with cuts and bruises and black eyes, his knuckles permanently skinned. There was pretty much no one he wouldn't throw a punch at, given the chance.

But on a horse? Drea suddenly became a giant goddamn chicken. Sure, he'd move his mallet if the ball was just sitting there, plump and pretty, and no one else was coming for it, but other than that very unlikely scenario, the guy was a total pussy on the field. He was afraid of falling, he was afraid of getting bumped off his horse, he was afraid of the ball hitting him in the face, and most especially, he was afraid of leaning out. And you can't play polo if you won't lean out.

"Drea, move!" I yelled as their back took the ball and thundered toward their goal, but Drea just loped along like he was taking his first pony ride in the park.

Another goal for the opposing team, and the end of the first chukker. Time to switch ponies. We rode out of the arena on our sweating, steaming mounts to the sound of unenthusiastic applause.

"Listen, you guys," Lezlie coached us as we swung up onto our new ponies. "They're only four ahead. We can still come back. Drea, you need to take a swing once in a while."

"What do you mean? I always take my swing!" He protested with such heat that, for a moment, I was afraid he was going to take that swing at Lezlie herself.

She ignored him. "And Gerb—mind your temper. It doesn't help anyone if you melt down on the field."

"I'm not melting down!" snapped Gerb.

"And you, Kareem," she said to me, and I knew what was coming. She said it to me every game. "You need to be a better captain. Delegate and stop trying to play for everyone else. You're out there playing defense and offense; you're all over the field. You have two teammates and they deserve a chance to step up, too."

"Right," I said, but I wasn't listening, not really. My head was already back in the arena figuring out how I could single-handedly get us out of this hole.

The next chukker was worse than the first; the opposing team replaced two of their players with their alternates, and the fresh riders made six more merciless goals against us. We managed nothing but a bunch of dumb moves, penalties, and near misses from our side. When the bell rang this time, we were hanging our heads in shame as we handed over our spent ponies to be hot-walked around the barn.

Lezlie was still coaching, but she wasn't giving us any more pep talks about catching up. She switched back over to her standard line of cheerful patter about how it didn't matter who won, it was just great that we even showed up to play. But her words didn't help. Our previous optimism had been trampled. We knew we were going to lose. Again. And we were pretty sure we were going to lose in the most humiliating kind of way. We were proving what we had feared from the beginning—that we were a joke. We had no right to be on that field. The only thing left to do was get on fresh horses and get this ass-kicking over with. It surely couldn't get any worse.

But of course, it did. Unlike the other team, we didn't have any alternates, so as they replaced player after player, each one of them bringing a fresh taste for our blood onto the field, we began to stumble and lag. And as we grew more tired, whatever small amount of patience Gerb had left rapidly began to dwindle.

Midway through the third chukker, when Drea refused another easy hit, Gerb got disgusted and came galloping over to chase the ball himself, but as he got closer, the umpire blew his whistle and called a foul.

"Impeding the right of way!" he shouted, waving his hands in the air.

"The fuck I did!" screamed Gerb.

Amidst a small wave of disapproving whispers from the audience, the umpire blew his whistle again. Additional penalty for language.

For a moment, I squeezed my eyes shut, hoping that when I opened them back up, Gerb would be done. But it was never that easy. I knew my brother. He was just getting started.

"Did you hear me, ump?"

The umpire rolled his eyes and looked away, ignoring Gerb. Gerb threw down his mallet and dug his heels into his horse's sides, galloping toward the umpire.

"I said, did you hear me?"

He was heading straight for the ump, like he was going to mow right into his mount.

Lezlie and I started screaming in unison. "Gerb! Gerb! Stop! STOP! What are you doing? GERB!"

Ten feet away from the umpire, Gerb pulled up his reins and brought his pony to a standstill, and for just a moment, I breathed a little easier, thinking maybe he'd come to his senses, maybe he'd just take the foul and we could keep playing. But then, the umpire blew his whistle again—and with a strangled yell, Gerb threw down his reins, jumped off his mount, and started heading for the guy on foot instead.

The players on the other team all came to a halt, watching in amazement as this tiny Black kid, no bigger than an average ten-year-old, came at the big, burly, white umpire like he thought he could knock him and his horse into the stands.

"I did not go over the motherfucking line, you asshole!" he screamed.

I knew my kid brother, and I knew that he had taken all he could take. The other team's merciless pounding, the embarrassment of losing by such a large margin, the inability to make even one goal . . . he was in the kind of red haze that almost nothing could pull him out of. He was really and truly going to attack this guy.

I spurred my horse on, hoping to get over there before we were all banned from polo for life.

The umpire blew his whistle over and over but Gerb kept coming. I rode as fast as I could. I could hear Drea laughing behind me. He always thought it was hilarious when Gerb melted down, happy that someone else besides him was getting in trouble for a change.

Finally we heard Lezlie's voice, louder than anything else in the arena.

"TIME OUT! Time out! Gerb, you're out! Get off the field! I'm pulling you from the game!"

Gerb came to an instant halt. Nothing else could have stopped him, but Lezlie's voice had somehow penetrated. He blinked his eyes for a moment, and then refocused his anger.

"What do you mean I'm out? What do you mean?"

"Get off the field, Gerb! You're done!" called Lezlie back at him.

Gerb practically danced with anger, but even in his most violent rages, he would never actually swear at Lezlie, so he redirected his gaze toward the ceiling instead. "FUCK THIS! Fuck this shit! Fucking fuck everyone!"

The ump kept blowing his whistle. Penalty after penalty.

I finally reached my brother. I pulled up my horse next to him. "Gerb," I said quietly. "Gerb. Look at me. Hey, bro. It's okay. Just get out of the arena."

He looked up at me, his eyes still snapping with rage, but then he blinked, and his face cleared and he suddenly looked like the little kid he really was. "Oh man," he whispered. "I'm sorry, Reem. I messed it up again, didn't I?"

I shrugged. "We were gonna lose anyway. Get off the field before Lezlie has to come out here and get you."

He bit his lip, and then nodded and started to head for the side.

"Your horse, Gerb!" yelled Lezlie, and he scurried back to grab his abandoned horse, who was still standing patiently midfield.

We played two-on-three for the rest of the game, but really

it felt like three-on-one, because Drea basically sat there glued to his saddle and acted like he was binge-watching Maury Povich instead of riding. Gerb and Lezlie silently observed from the sidelines, wincing as I raced desperately all over the field, trying to salvage our name and dignity, as the other team continued to run rings around us and rack up goal after goal.

———

We lost 32 to 0. One more defeat in an unbroken string of losses that season.

The crowd was silent when we finally rode off the field.

———

Three years later, the crowd was a different kind of quiet as I cantered up the field, keeping my eyes glued to the small white ball teed up in the dirt. Almost nobody made this kind of penalty shot. There were so many things that could go wrong. You could hit it low, a ground-burner that might catch in a divot and bounce off in the wrong direction. You might hit it nice and high, but the goal was three hundred feet away, so without the right power behind it, the ball could easily fall short. Your pony could stumble or hesitate, sneeze, or try to shake off an annoying fly. Someone in the crowd could distract you and throw you off your game. You could swing a fraction of a second too early or too late. You could be too in your head, or not paying enough attention, or you could try too hard. Everything had to line up exactly right: your horse had to glide, your form had to be perfect, your strength had to be just the right mix of powerful but controlled, and your aim had to be timely and true. This shot would win or lose the game, but getting it just right was as likely as winning the lotto.

I was galloping, but it felt like slow motion. I could hear my own breath, rasping in and out. I could feel each singular thud of my pony's hooves as they hit the ground, and the corresponding beat of my own heart that accompanied it. The ball loomed bigger and bigger as I got closer and closer, and then, just as I had almost passed it by, I lifted my mallet and swung, bringing the head down to kiss the ball and then finishing up in a swift 360-degree arc through the air.

It felt good. In fact, it felt like a goddamned near-perfect strike, but I still held my breath, waiting to see where it would land. The ball went flying into the sky like a rocket, heading up and up, lofty and straight, over the heads of the watching players, easily outdistancing them as they galloped along below it.

The lights of the stadium were bright and I squinted, trying to track the ball's flight. For a moment, I couldn't find it. I had the strange feeling that I'd sent it so far, that it had flown so damned high, that it had gone into orbit and might not actually return. The crowd seemed to hold its breath with me, and then, all at once, the ball came whistling down, soaring through the air and dropping right into the goal. The arc was so graceful, the aim was so true; it reminded me of the way a stone slices into the sea.

My breath burst out of my lungs with a ragged gasp and the crowd exploded along with me. It didn't matter who they wanted to win; seeing a two-point goal was like watching a hole-in-one or a home run. If you were a fan of the game, you appreciated how magical and rare the moment was.

"Yes! Yes! Fucking YES!" Gerb was screaming at the top of his lungs as he charged back into the lineup. I held up my mallet, laughing wildly as my little brother rode by, holding his own mallet aloft so we could cross sticks with a satisfying crash—the polo player's version of a high five or a touchdown dance. We were still riding, there was a little time left on the clock, and it was only the beginning of the season, but, just this once, we were celebrating early. We all knew it was over. We knew that we'd already won.

CHAPTER ONE

It always started at a low rumble, drifting through our bedroom wall.

I would pull my pillow (if I was lucky enough to have one that night; otherwise, my coat or whatever else I happened to be sleeping on) up over my head, hoping that if I blocked out the sound, it meant that it would stop.

But it almost never stopped.

Soon enough, the rumble would increase in volume, becoming sharper and more distinct, until it very clearly became two human voices—the low, harsh tones of my mother's most recent boyfriend, and the higher, angry and frightened sound of my mother.

The pillow didn't help anymore. Neither did the blanket that I would pull up over the pillow. Their voices only grew louder, throwing around accusations and curses, calling each other bitch and asshole, hurling insults and threats . . . they might as well have been standing right there in the room with us.

All six of us kids would be awake by then: David and Bee, me and Kareema, Gerb and baby Washika, all holding our breaths and squeezing our eyes shut and hoping against hope that somehow what we knew was coming next just wouldn't happen this time.

But it always did.

A smack. A crash. The sound of a fist hitting flesh. Broken glass. A shout. A scream. The door smashing open and the thud of a body falling to the floor, sometimes tumbling down the stairs.

We'd huddle like baby mice in a nest, quaking and crying as we listened to the sound of our mother's screams. Until her voice would finally hit a note that was so desperate and pleading that we wouldn't be able to stand it anymore and we'd all tumble out into the hall as one, blinking our eyes in the bright light, moving in a herd toward the bathroom where he had his knees pinned down on our mother's arms, one hand over her mouth, forcing her head down onto the floor next to the toilet—her legs kicking desperately, her dark eyes wide with fear—the other hand in his pocket, grasping his gun and telling her he was going to fucking shove it in her mouth and shoot her fucking bitch brains out.

—

Later, after our next-door neighbor called the cops and the boyfriend finally got off my mother, and my mother—with blood dripping from her mouth, and a bruise already forming on her cheek, with her hands still trembling and her voice coming out in a strangled, raspy whisper—answered the door and insisted that everything was fine and refused to press charges—later, after all that, the boyfriend lined us up and sheepishly handed out five- and ten-dollar bills like he always did. It was his way of proving that he wasn't really a monster, that he took care of all these kids that weren't even his. He told us that he was sorry that we'd had to see what our mother had forced him to do to her again.

——

When my mother, Lazette, was a little girl, she was fast and strong. Faster and stronger than any of the boys in her class. She didn't like to hang out with girls. She would rather run races down her street and play football in the vacant lot with the neighborhood boys. She played basketball and climbed trees and jumped fences. She had dreams that maybe if she was strong enough and fast enough, she might somehow run right out of The Bottom.

But my mom was also beautiful, with her brown, flashing eyes and wide, warm smile. Pretty soon the boys who used to race against her and tumble around with her in the park started seeing her in a brand-new way.

She had her first baby, David, when she was fourteen years old. My mother loved her new son, but the adjustment from being a child to being a mother was brutal. At first, she wanted to continue to act like a kid, slipping away to hang out with her friends after her baby fell asleep, messing around on the street corner, but her mother, Sheila, was not having any of that. She insisted that her daughter stay home and care for her baby, and when my mom didn't listen, my grandma would march on out and drag her home by the ear if necessary.

Even after my mother had David, my mom still thought there might be a way out—that maybe she could be strong enough to carry him with her. But then, not more than a year later, she had her second baby, and then four more of us—with three different men, none of whom had a hand in raising us—all before she turned thirty. And as every kid came along, the losses started piling up. Her sister died of AIDS. One of her brothers was shot dead in the street; the other lost his legs to diabetes. It became clear that it didn't matter how strong or fast my mother once was; we were too heavy a responsibility. There was no way out, and the only thing left that she could possibly do for us was teach us all how to survive right where we were.

—

My mother never let us go hungry; there was always food in our house. We had new clothes and shoes when we really needed them, and she made sure we went to the doctor and the dentist. And we always had a roof over our heads, even if all six of us had to share a room and a bed, or sometimes sleep on the floor. She had an open-door policy; cousins and aunts and uncles, friends and friends of friends, anytime anyone asked, they could stay with us, as long as they needed. Even if it meant that we kids were pushed out of our beds, even if it meant stretching things as far as they would stretch and then some. Sometimes we wouldn't have heat or hot water, but she'd boil water on the stovetop so we could bathe, tell us to put on our coats and hats and mittens, hang sheets over the entryways, and turn on the oven in the kitchen and let it warm up as much of the first floor as it could. We'd all sleep in a puppy pile on the living-room floor, our breaths puffing out in little white clouds, but our hands and toes warm from the body heat of seven of us curled up against each other.

My mother hustled to take care of the basics in every way she could. She always had at least one job. Minimum wage. She'd dropped out of school when she got pregnant at thirteen, so her options were limited. Fast food, janitorial work, the corner store. She also had her weekly welfare checks. And she had the occasional boyfriend, most of whom she kept around much longer than she should. Even after they turned mean, even after they hurt her, even after things started to burn down around her and fall to pieces.

When I was a kid, I used to wonder why she stayed with these guys, how she could stand it, but now I can see that our food, our shoes, our dental and doctor bills, the rent, the utilities, the never-ending needs of six children, it all had to be paid for somehow, and these guys contributed. And really, she was not much more than a kid herself. She was growing up alongside us. These men were older and wiser, she thought. She says that they were helping her mature. She says she loved them, or at least, loved some of them. But sometimes I wonder if the real truth was that our mother stayed because we needed so much, and these men sometimes came through with money for us when she couldn't, and if that meant she took a beating, it was worth it to her.

———

The six (seven if you included my mom) of us grew up in West Philadelphia on Viola Street. Think block upon block of narrow row houses, some filled to the brim with family and extended family, some boarded up or burned down, leaving a space in the row like a missing tooth in a smile. There weren't any gangs in our neighborhoods, but you had your people based on where you lived and maybe a five-block radius in every direction around that. That was your safe zone. If you had blood relatives—cousins or aunties or uncles— who lived farther out, you might be okay on their block, too. But other than that, you stuck to your streets, your neighborhood, and knew the consequences if you drifted too far abroad.

Parents in our neighborhood had two choices when it came to raising their kids. They could try to make them safe by keeping them locked up, by taking them by the hand and walking them to school, and doing their best to steer them away from the drugs and sex and guns and violence that were right out there on street for anyone to see. They could whisk them home at the end of the day and lock their doors and pull their curtains and not even talk about what was out there. Or they could do what our mother did, which was to take us everywhere and let us see everything up close. We saw the drug dealers and the prostitutes and the guns and the makeshift altars of wooden crosses and scattered flowers on the street that meant someone had been killed there. We saw the knock-down, drag-out fights and people smoking crack and men drinking in the empty lots. We saw women selling themselves for drug money and men hustling on the corners. From the time we were babies, our mom would throw open our door and we'd come out trailing after her into the streets like ducklings in a row, and she'd introduce us to it all, letting us talk to these people and watch it all up close and hoping that by making us see how she dealt with it—showing us the danger—we would turn hard enough and smart enough to know what to do when we inevitably had to face all that stuff alone.

It was no surprise that with all the pressure in her life—the neighborhood and the money worries and the shitty jobs, the violent men and the never-ending needs of six kids—my mother had to find ways to escape. She often disappeared with the men she dated, sometimes for days at a time. Left us with our grandmother or an older cousin, or on our own once my big brothers hit an age where they could keep track of us all. And even when she was home, she let us run wild; with no curfew, no rules to follow, the only time she corrected us was when she didn't get her own way. We had good home training, we knew how to be polite and say "yes, sir" and "no, ma'am," we had some table manners and knew to say please and thanks, but the rest was left up to us—whether we went to school, whether we came home at night, who we ran with, what we did with our time. I was a mama's boy, but even I learned quick that I could only depend on my brothers and sisters and myself, that my mom only had so much she could give. She was practically a kid herself, and we needed so much. Trying to keep us all in line on top of just trying to keep us safe and alive was more than most anyone could handle.

She had other ways to escape. She was a functional addict, coke and weed and booze, for as long as I could remember. She'd bring strangers and friends into the house at night and we'd wake up to the thick skunky smell of last night's weed in the air, empty crack vials strewn on the kitchen table, tipped-over beer bottles dripping their last dregs onto the floor.

She didn't use all the time, but I hated it when she did. I could always tell when she'd been partying because even if she was physically there, she was absent in almost every other way, sitting on the couch, her eyes dull and her face slack. I'd ask her a simple question and her response would be delayed just enough to let me know that she wasn't present, that once again, she had chosen the drugs over us.

She sobered up sometimes. She'd go to Narcotics Anonymous and swear she was turning over a new leaf. For a month or two, she'd stay home with us, clear eyed and aware. But then, something unbearably bad would happen like it always did; she'd lose her job, or someone we knew and loved would get shot, or she'd find a new man who was just as much of an asshole as the last man she'd been with. And she couldn't run fast anymore, so she'd have to find another way out.

———

Viola Street wasn't all bad. There was a sense of everyone being in it together. If you needed to borrow money for gas or food or rent, and your neighbor had a few extra bills, you could be sure they'd give it to you. The children played in the streets and the adults didn't hesitate to call you out if you were doing something foolish, even if you weren't their kid. Most doors were open and everyone knew each other's business and when something went wrong, they helped when they could, because we were all in the same barely floating boat, and if we didn't have each other, we didn't have anyone.

My siblings and I made up our own little group. We ran in the streets like our mom once had, playing basketball at the schoolyard and football in the empty lots. We poked around in puddles and through the grass, looking for frogs and bugs; we caught fireflies in the summer and threw snowballs in the winter. Even in a place as full of need and violence as our neighborhood was, even with our mom getting beat up, even with her and my grandmother using, our fathers nothing more than drunk strangers we passed on the street every once in a while, we were still children, and there was still joy.

But we never forgot that we were in a dangerous place. We saw people get beaten up by the cops, buying and selling on the street corners, shot down where they were standing. We lost people, over and over, uncles and cousins and friends. Dying young was just the way things were.

And we knew that even if we managed to survive, we'd just end up living through the same hard times, the same fear, the same need, that our mother had been living her whole life. And so, on those cold winter nights, when we were all huddled up together on the living-room floor, trying to sleep, we'd whisper to each other about how our family was going to be different. How our family was going to get out.

We just didn't know how yet.

CHAPTER TWO

It was my big brothers David and Bee who first found the Work to Ride stables. David was twelve and Bee was ten. As they tell it, they were riding their bikes on a gray and cold Sunday morning when they decided to explore Fairmount Park, a huge swath of green space only twenty minutes from our neighborhood. They took a turn at a dead-end road that they'd never been down before and screeched to a stop, staring at the long, curved lines and vine-covered walls of a sprawling and worn-down barn. Fenced corrals were on both sides, and inside the corrals—heads bent to the ground, moving slowly through the mist as they grazed—were the horses.

My family loved animals. We were always dragging home stray dogs and feeding mangy cats, hiding half a dozen snapping turtles in our back shed, capturing frogs and snakes, putting whatever insects we could find into empty tomato-sauce jars stuffed full of grass and leaves, and then begging our mom to let us keep whatever poor creature we'd carried through the back door. When our dog Tummy (so named because she had a swollen belly full of worms when I found her) first came home, I would wake up early each morning and creep into my mom's room, quietly cleaning up whatever mess the dog had left in the night before my mom could open her eyes and see it and decide Tummy was more trouble than she was worth.

But horses were our favorites.

Even if you're not from Philly, I'm sure you've heard of the Liberty Bell and cheesesteaks and Will Smith. You probably know all about Ben Franklin, the City of Brotherly Love, and the Declaration of Independence. But there are also some things you probably don't know about my city. You might be surprised to learn that less than a ten-minute drive from the Ivy League campus of University of Pennsylvania there are neighborhoods so messed up that any baby boy born there has a good chance at either being shot or incarcerated by the time he turns twenty. You might not know that Philly has one of the highest poverty rates in the U.S. or that many of our public schools are desperately starved for funds.

But the thing that seems to shock most people about Philadelphia, above all else, is when I tell them about the horses in our neighborhood.

Imagine walking down an inner-city block; there are the usual *papi* stores (our name for bodegas), folks sitting out on their stoops and hanging on the street corners, men drinking in empty lots and kids running wild, and then, out of nowhere, a Black man comes charging down the street on a full-grown horse.

In my neighborhood, that could happen anytime.

There is a history of horses and horsemanship in The Bottom that goes back a century or more. Men who still call themselves Black Cowboys keep horses in their tiny backyard sheds or garages, they graze them in empty lots, they ride them through the streets and race them down the Speedway (a long stretch of uneven path in Fairmount Park), making bets on the winners. Some of these guys have created clubs made up of a few horses that were on their way to being turned into dog food when they saved them from the livestock auctions in New Holland. They'd bring them home, fatten them up, and then welcome in kids from the streets to learn to groom and ride.

Kids in our neighborhood might not ever learn to swim or be offered much of an education, we might see way more bad shit, way too young, than any kid ever should, but most of us had taken advantage of the cheap pony rides offered in the neighborhood and at least sat on a horse by the time we started walking. Most of us know what the staccato beat of hooves hitting the concrete sounds like. Most of us have had the chance to feel the way a horse will blow his warm breath into your hand if you cup it to his nose. And when you're around horses like that, even when you're in a neighborhood as hard as ours was, you can't help falling a little bit in love.

Or at least that's what happened to me and my brothers.

Back in the park and mesmerized by the ponies, my brothers abandoned their bikes and crept up the path toward the barn, absolutely sure they were going to get shouted at and chased off at any moment. They stuck their heads in through the barn door, taking their first deep breath of that sweet, acrid smell of hay and manure and dampness and mud, and the unmistakable warm, musky scent of the horses themselves.

They took one step in, and then another, silently daring each other on until they turned the corner. Then they stopped, wide eyed and shocked.

The stable was full of kids. Kids shoveling out stalls, kids carrying flakes of hay, kids currying their ponies, saddling up and then leading them out of the barn; some kids so young that they could hardly lift a shovel or reach their horse's mane. And all these kids looked like my brothers, they looked like they were from our part of the hood. David and Bee didn't know what to think. They kept looking around, trying to find the adult in charge. It was like some strange fairytale where children had magically taken over the village.

"Hey, you two."

Bee and David almost jumped out of their skins when a stern-looking white lady with long blond hair rounded the corner and caught them both standing there, mouths hanging open.

They turned in unison, ready to run.

"You guys want to meet the horses?" she asked.

———

Bee came home that night with a chunk out of his face where a horse named Devil had reached over the fence and bitten him. He had a big white bandage on his cheek, and would end up with a livid scar, but he didn't care. He and David had found the best place in the world, he declared, and the lady who ran it said that if they kept their grades up and stayed out of trouble, they could come back every day and she'd teach them to ride for free.

I was wild with jealousy. I wanted to be where my big

brothers were. There were not a lot of men in my life. My father was a stranger who spent his days drinking in a vacant lot around the corner from where we lived. I used to pass right by him on an almost daily basis and he never even so much as nodded at me. I was close to my mother and my grandmother, but I craved the attention of my big brothers so bad it made me itch.

Even before my brothers found the barn, they weren't around the house much anymore. They were gone more than not, but at least I still had access to them. If they were just hanging out in the neighborhood, they'd sometimes let me tag along, and even when they didn't, it was easy enough to find them when I wanted to. They couldn't go far. But once they started going to Work to Ride, they were out of my range. There was no tracking them down; they were just gone. And I was stuck at home with Kareema and Gerb and Washika—a bunch of babies, as far as I was concerned.

I begged David and Bee to take me with them, but they just shook their heads and laughed.

"You're not big enough," said Bee.

"And you're a little punk, basically afraid of everything," said David.

They weren't wrong. I was scared shitless of pretty much everything. Unlike my fearless brothers who always dove in headfirst, I preferred to hang back and watch from afar, get a full measure of the situation before I decided to get involved. I was all eyes and ears. And if something seemed even remotely dangerous (which, let's face it, most everything in our lives was) I would walk half a dozen blocks out of my way to avoid it altogether. Those teeth marks on Bee's cheek would normally have been enough to keep me home, but I couldn't stand my brothers' absence. I pestered them endlessly, and when they wouldn't give in, I pulled out the big guns and started whining to my mom instead. It took about two weeks to wear her down, but she finally told my brothers that if they didn't take me with them, they couldn't go at all.

They were probably pissed that they had to drag me along that first morning, but all I remember about that day was just how happy and excited I was. They had been talking about nothing else but the barn and riding for weeks now, and I already felt like I knew every horse in the place. I was shivering as we made the twenty-minute walk from our neighborhood to the stables, but I couldn't tell you if it was from the early winter cold, or if it was from excitement, because I was with my big brothers and we were going to the place they described as a paradise.

—

Angel was the first pony I ever rode. She was everyone's first pony. She was a small, shaggy, iron-gray horse with dark eyes and a sweet disposition. She was also about a million years old and guaranteed to patiently put up with any beginning rider that was placed upon her swayed back. She never really felt like breaking into anything faster than a slow trot, and she was an expert at teaching new students. Even so, when David led her out of her stall and Bee handed me a curry mitt, I stood there staring at that easygoing pony like she might turn wild at any moment and trample me in a crazy equine rage.

"Oh, come on, don't punk out," said David. "She's not going to hurt you."

"She's like a big dog," agreed Bee. "Just give her a pat."

Not wanting to embarrass myself in front of my brothers,

I took a step forward and hesitantly reached to touch Angel's flank, jumping back when she quivered a little and snorted.

Bee shoved me forward again. "If you want to ride, you have to learn to groom," he said.

Honestly, I wasn't sure I wanted to ride. Angel was a small pony, but I was an even smaller kid, and to me, she looked looming and dangerous. But as my brothers stood there watching me with big, anticipatory grins on their faces, I did know for sure that I didn't want to disappoint them, so I reached my hand out again.

Horses are softer than you think they're going to be; their coats are silky and smooth, the hair on their muzzles feels like velvet, their sensitive ears twitch and shiver under your fingers. They smell good, too. Like sweet hay and molasses from their feed, like tender grass and clover. They have an animal musk, but it's the musk of a prey animal, not a predator, honeyed and warm.

Both of my brothers taught me how to groom and tack up that day, but Bee was more patient than David. It had always been that way. Maybe just because Bee was closer to me in age. Or maybe because Bee knew that there was no one else in the world that I looked up to like I looked up to him. Both of my brothers were smart, strong, and fearless, but David was grown up enough to already have one foot out the door; he didn't have a lot of use for another kid brother. Bee, on the other hand, always had my back.

Bee recited the parts of the pony as he showed me how to rub the grooming mitt over Angel's body: *muzzle, forehead, poll, crest, withers* . . . I felt her coat soften as it started to shine under my hands. He demonstrated how to carefully untangle her mane and tail, slowly easing through each knot and kink.

How I needed to trail my fingers down her legs, searching for any bumps or cuts, making sure she was sound. He had me watch as he picked her front hooves, then let me do her back ones. I couldn't believe the way that animal was so quick to offer up her feet and trust me to care for her.

After we were done grooming, David handed me a tiny Western saddle and a bridle, and Bee showed me how to tack up. I was too scared of her big, yellow teeth to put the bit in her mouth, so Bee did it, but I was so proud when Angel dipped her head and let me pull the bridle up over her ears. I reached up to pat her again, loving the way she nuzzled against my hand, hoping for a treat.

"You ready to ride?" asked Bee after David helped me strap on a borrowed helmet. I didn't have any riding gear. I was wearing jeans and tennis shoes and only had a pair of knitted mittens, no gloves, but I didn't care or know any better. Everything about this experience was new to me, and so far it had all been wonderful.

Still, as I climbed up the mounting block and David told me to swing my leg over Angel's back, I couldn't help but wish that the pony had been a little closer to the ground. Angel did not feel like I expected; she was both bigger and bonier than I'd imagined, and when David took the reins and started leading me out to the ring, I clung to the saddle horn and fought the urgent desire to jump off as she lumbered and swayed under me.

All I did that day was take a pony ride, pretty much the same as you might take at a child's birthday party or petting zoo. David slowly led me round the ring, never letting go of the reins or letting Angel go faster than a slow, jerky trot that rattled my teeth and other, more unmentionable, parts.

But I was terrified, imagining all the things that could go wrong. What if Angel reared up (never mind that this elderly horse obviously no longer had the strength to do more than slowly make her way around the ring) or scraped me off and trampled me? What if she broke free of her reins and took off running? What if she jumped the fence? Or reached back and bit me with those big yellow teeth? The ride was filled with horrible possibilities.

But of course, none of those things happened. Led by David, Angel just walked and then slowly trotted and then walked again, me jouncing helplessly along on her back as she circled the ring. And then, before I knew it, the ride was over and Bee was helping me dismount, and suddenly I was back on the ground and my legs were shaking and my head hurt a little, and I was absolutely filled with the urgent need *to do it all again.*

I know I must have met Lezlie that day; she wouldn't have let a new kid into the stable without introducing herself and going over the rules with them first, but honestly, in my memory, it was just me and David and Bee and Angel. There were surely other kids there, too, but in my mind, we had the entire stable to ourselves. We had claimed the barn, and everything in it, as ours.

That feeling of ownership never left me, but it soon became starkly obvious that there were rules to go along with it. A lot of rules. Lezlie Hiner made it very clear that you best not mess with her or her stable, or you'd be out on your ass.

Lezlie had been horse crazy ever since she was a little girl growing up as the eldest of four sisters. She said if you took her to the store, you better have had a nickel for the mechanical horse so she could ride. Her family didn't have a lot of money, but Lez always found a way to be around horses. When she was younger, she'd work odd jobs to earn enough cash to rent a hack horse and teach herself as she rode over the trails. When she was fifteen, someone gave her uncle, who was a country doctor, a little bay mare as payment for his services. Knowing how much Lezlie loved horses, and not having any use for the animal himself, the uncle offered the pony to his niece. Lezlie's father agreed that she could have the mare, but only if she worked enough to pay for half the board and care. Lezlie happily put in thirty hours a week at the stable to keep up her end of the bargain.

Once Lezlie graduated from high school, she found ways to keep working with horses. She started at a horse farm doing chores, and then got a job as a hot-walker at the racetrack, and later moved up to groom. As a groom, she traveled all over the U.S. with trainers, only stopping in South Carolina when she decided to go to college and earn her degree in psychology. After graduation, she thought that maybe she needed a more respectable job, so she returned to Philly and worked for her father at his record storage business, sorting and keeping track of files. But she still rode every chance she got, and soon enough she knew she had to find another way to make horses her life. It was all she ever wanted.

Every weekend, she'd go to a local stable with her friends to ride. Saturday was the work day, cleaning and grooming, and Sunday was the ride day, when she would take advantage of the vast network of trails that ran through Philly's Fairmount Park. One day, she noticed a little Black kid, barely older than nine, who was hanging around the stables, watching Lezlie and her friends load up their horses. His name was Carl. The farrier who worked at the barn had brought him along as a favor to Carl's mom.

Carl returned now and then, helping the farrier when he could, and quietly watching Lezlie and her friends as they laughed and joked and loaded up their horses for their weekly ride. Finally, one day, as they were leaving the barnyard, Lezlie looked into her rearview mirror and saw him standing there watching them as they drove away.

Lezlie didn't like to stop for much, but she said that the look on the kid's face was so lonely and wistful that she swore under her breath, hit the brakes, got out, and went back into the barn to grab another pony.

Every Sunday after that, Carl rode with Lezlie. He became a fixture at the barn, and she taught him everything she knew about horses. Carl was from Dogtown, a rough part of Philly, and was one of four kids with a single mom. He was shy and wary and Lezlie saw how the horses gave him purpose and focus and hope. She saw how his confidence blossomed as he became a horseman.

The part of her that had trained in psychology also saw the therapeutic possibilities between horses and kids. She loved Philly, but it was clear to her that there was a vast group of traumatized and underserved children living in the city she called home. She wanted to do more.

When she was thirty-seven, her dad fired her from her job. She was distracted, he said, and not taking her work seriously. Lezlie always said he did her the biggest favor of her life, because by the time she was thirty-eight, she had drawn up a business plan and convinced the city of Philadelphia to lease her the run-down Chamounix Stables in Fairmount Park for a dollar. She contacted everyone she knew in the horse world, working every angle she could think of, until she cobbled together a group of ex-racehorses and donated ponies, old tack and equipment, and enough money to buy feed and bedding for a month or two. She opened the doors to Work to Ride in 1994.

—

By the time us Rosser kids arrived, Lezlie had a set of hard-and-fast rules. Work to Ride was exactly what we had to do. You showed up every day after school and early on the weekend, you mucked out the stalls and brushed down your pony, you picked their hooves and untangled their tails, you made sure your animal was fed and watered, you washed your bridle and rubbed down your saddle, you swept up the piles of hair and dirt you created while trying to get your horse clean, and then, and only then, were you actually allowed to take your horse out and ride. And if Lezlie made her walk-through and discovered that you had skipped over even one of those steps? She didn't think twice about yanking you off your horse, marching you back into the barn, and standing over you with a ferocious look on her face until everything was as it should be. And those were just the barn rules. In order to stay in the program, you also had to keep no lower than a C average in school (and bring Lezlie the report cards to prove it), keep your nose out of trouble on the streets, and commit to all this work and responsibility for at least a year, with the underlying expectation that, if you were lucky, you would stay on until you graduated from high school.

The Rosser kids didn't care. We would have signed everything in our own blood if it meant we got our hands on a horse. We promised whatever we had to promise, and convinced our mom that it was perfectly safe. David didn't have the grades to get in, so he doctored a copy of Gerb's kindergarten report card and made it look like it was his. (Lezlie wasn't fooled at all, but she told us later that she figured a kid who wanted in that bad ought to get a chance to ride and do better.) We were expected to write a three-hundred-word essay explaining why we wanted to be part of the program. Since I could barely read or write when I joined the barn, this was a particular challenge for me, but one I met nonetheless, rambling on in a barely legible scrawl about how I loved horses and I wanted to be with my brothers and learn to ride like a pro.

I would have done just about anything to be part of this new world we had stumbled into. Maybe I didn't have the words for it yet, but I instinctually knew that the barn was safer, *better,* than home—an island in the middle of all the trouble that we couldn't escape otherwise. And I was determined to do anything I could to keep coming back.

CHAPTER THREE

The average American, if they think about polo at all, thinks the game is all about billionaires and royalty, Veuve Clicquot and stomping divots. They probably think about that scene in *Pretty Woman*: Julia Roberts in gloves and a fancy hat surrounded by a bunch of rich assholes. Polo is called *the sport of kings,* and we've all seen Prince Harry done up in his white jeans and leather kneepads enough times to understand why.

But most people don't understand the game. They don't know about the speed and the danger and the incredible rush of riding a horse at thirty miles per hour. They don't know about the bloodthirsty competition and the way you sometimes feel like you might actually die—horses and their riders thundering on either side of you, trying to knock you out of the way—as you stretch as far as you can reach, hanging halfway off your pony, to hit that tiny ball. They don't know that many players actually *do* die; that next to NASCAR, polo has the highest fatality rate of any sport. People also can't imagine that moment when you and your mount become one singular creature and he's reading your mind and making the right moves before you can even fully form them in your head. They don't know what it feels like to make contact and smash that ball into oblivion, sending it so far and so fast that, for a moment, it disappears from view.

Before Work to Ride, I didn't know all that, either. In fact, I didn't even know that polo existed.

As far as I was concerned, polo was basically invented when I found the barn. I didn't know about all the trappings and ceremony and reputation around it. I had no idea that, in the U.S., polo was a sport pretty much reserved for very wealthy, very privileged white people. The first time I saw polo, it wasn't from the bleachers of an exclusive club, it was being played by a bunch of scrawny-ass Black kids galloping some secondhand horses around a soccer field, mallets in hand, chasing a dirty ball. It might as well have been a pickup game of touch football or red light-green light. It just looked like a fun time to me.

"Yo, what's that?" I asked Bee.

"It's polo," he said, and the reverence and awe in his voice made me look again. My brother already sounded like a fanatic.

—

Before we were allowed to play polo, we had to learn to ride. Lezlie wasn't letting anyone pick up a mallet before she trusted their horsemanship. Riding came easy to David and especially Bee, but as usual, my particular set of fears and anxieties caused me to lag behind. My brothers were off the lead line in days, trotting and then cantering within weeks, moving up to more and more challenging horses, and then finally out with the bigger kids, on that soccer field, mallets in hand. Me, I was staying firmly on Angel, plodding relentlessly around the ring, determined not to do anything that might end up with me hitting the ground.

Sometimes I'd watch my brothers, riding like demons, big old grins on their faces as they chased that little ball, and I'd feel a twinge of longing and wish just a tiny bit that I could get out there, too, but then I'd give a shrug, climb right back up on Angel, and resume our slow-ass trot. I was at the barn with my brothers, I got to ride a horse, and, as far as I was concerned, that was plenty.

—

One morning we got to the barn and Lezlie came to meet us at the door. She looked even more stern than usual, and I frantically thought back through the previous day, worried I'd done something wrong.

"Guys," she said, putting her hand on my shoulder, "I'm afraid that I have some very bad news. Angel colicked last night. We called the vet, but we couldn't save her. She's gone."

Now, under normal circumstances, I would have been really sad. I loved animals, and over the months that I'd been at the barn, I'd grown extremely attached to Angel. I was in charge of her care and grooming. She always perked up when she saw me, snorting happily and nuzzling at my hands and neck, knowing that her grain and hay weren't far behind. She was sweet and easy and she carried me like I was precious cargo. She was my pony. But instead of crying for the loss of my friend, I was instantly paralyzed with fear. Because

I knew that if Angel was gone, I was going to have to ride another horse, and if I rode another horse, there was every chance in the world I was going to fall off.

Lezlie led us over to Angel's motionless body in the field so we could say goodbye, but I could barely look at her. My heart was pounding and all I could think about was which horse Lezlie would give me to ride next and whether or not I would actually be able to bring myself to get up on that horse, and if I couldn't actually ride that horse, would that mean I'd have to leave the barn?

I didn't ride that day, what with Lezlie having to deal with all the other kids (who were honestly, actually, sad and not selfishly spinning out like a puppy hiding the fact that he'd pissed on the floor) and having to arrange for the disposal of Angel's corpse. I methodically cleaned Angel's empty stall, unable to focus on the fact that this would be the last time I took care of her in this way, and then I climbed up into the hayloft and waited for my brothers to be done for the day, making myself as small and quiet as possible so that Lezlie wouldn't notice me and do something crazy like try to assign me a new horse.

I slipped out of the barn that night, grateful that she seemed to have forgotten all about me. But of course Lezlie never forgot about any of us, and the moment I walked in the next day, she was there waiting for me.

"How you doing, Kareem?" she said, giving me a smile.

I gulped. "I'm cool," I lied.

"I know you must miss Angel a lot, but she would have wanted you to keep riding, don't you think?"

I felt my eyes go big with fear. "I don't know about that."

"Well, I do," said Lezlie, nodding firmly. "So let's get you set up with Buck."

Buck. It couldn't have been worse. Buck was a big brown and white paint, a gelding, and he had his name for a reason. He loved to throw kids off. He'd play it cool at first, responding to your every request, happily walking and trotting and cantering at your command, but then, inevitably, he'd get this wild look in his eyes, and suddenly, with no warning at all, he'd just stop, and send you flying over his neck, or he'd rear up, or kick his back legs out. If you somehow managed to find a way to stick even after all that—he'd head for the nearest tree with a low-hanging branch and scrape you off like you were shit on his shoe.

There was no way in hell I was getting on Buck.

"No," I said. "No, thank you."

Lezlie looked at me. "Oh," she said. She sounded amused. "This isn't a choice, my friend. I'm assigning him to you. He's your horse now. So go put him in the corral and then you can clean out his stall, and once you're done with that, I'll give you a lesson."

I stared up at her for a moment, trying to decide whether I could beg or argue my way out of this, but it was Lezlie, and I already knew that once she made up her mind, that was it. If I wanted to stay at the barn, I would have to do as she said.

Every horse in our barn had issues. That was how we ended up with them. People donated them to us because they were old or too green, or they were worn out or wild or dumb, but Lezlie was a good trainer and she was even better at matching up horse to rider. She had an instinct about which horse would help which kid and vice versa. And for some reason

I could not fathom, she had picked out the one horse in the barn that I was most afraid of.

Buck wasn't a mean horse, exactly. He just had the bad habit of throwing kids off his back. In almost every other way, he was great. He bent his head and stood placidly, flicking his tail, as I slid on his halter, and he happily let me lead him out of his stall and turn him out in the corral where he went about his job of grazing, and shitting, and minding his own business. You could put him in with anyone. He got along with all the other horses, even the really nasty ones. But he was a horse, not a pony, and stood what felt like twice as high as Angel had, and of course I knew exactly what he was capable of.

I never cleaned a stall so thoroughly, or shined my boots and saddle with such care. I didn't miss a spot on the bridle, either. I figured that if I went slow enough, I might manage to run out the clock. But Lezlie caught on quick, and before I knew it, she had led Buck back in and was helping me tack him up.

I thought I would throw up, I was so nervous. I had seen dozens of kids fall off their horses by now, including both of my brothers, and though no one had been badly hurt, I had decided right away that it was not something I was going to experience if I could avoid it. For months, Angel, with her age and patience, had kept me safe; but my time had finally come. Buck was all tacked up and Lezlie was standing there, waiting. I led that horse over to the mounting block like it was my last day on earth.

My fall came almost at once, and amazingly, it had nothing to do with Buck. It was entirely my own fault. Not used to the bigger horse, I hadn't yanked his girth tight enough, and so we didn't take more than a few steps before my saddle slid out from under me, slipping to Buck's side. I rolled along with it, and was suddenly perpendicular to his back, suspended for just a moment before I fell off him in what felt like slow motion. It was a long way to the ground and I hit the dirt with a loud smack, landing face side up, with the wind knocked out of me.

Lezlie's face appeared above me. "You okay?" she asked.

I couldn't speak yet, but I managed to nod.

She grinned. "Good. Then fix your girth and get back on your horse."

I shook my head. No way.

She raised her eyebrows, and then firmly offered me her hand. It wasn't an offer so much as a command.

I hesitated, wondering if it was too late to work up some tears, but Lezlie had that look on her face, the one that said there was nothing to do but obey her. So I took her hand, and before I knew it, I was trotting around the ring, and maybe Buck felt that one fall was enough, because he didn't mess with me anymore that day at all.

—

I rode Buck every day after that. And I fell off many times. But I never got too hurt, and Lezlie was always there to help me back up again, and once I had fallen a dozen or so times, I realized that it wasn't that big a deal. Even if I did fall, I could just get back up and keep riding. And unlike Angel, Buck challenged me, he pushed me as a rider. He was never going to be content to crawl around the ring. He wanted to be big and bold, he wanted to have fun. And I think he wanted me to have fun, too. So one day, when he suddenly broke into a canter, something I had been fervently avoiding since day one, instead of sawing at the reins and trying desperately to make him stop, I sat deep in my saddle, softened up my body, and let him run.

—

It wasn't long after that Lezlie put a mallet into my hands and pointed me in the direction of the soccer field.

"It's time," she said. "You're ready."

I gripped the handle and took a tentative swing, clumsily imitating the move I had seen my brothers make a thousand times before.

I didn't do it right—the whole mallet almost flew out of my hand—but I felt an electric swoop of excitement down to my very bones. I knew what was next, and I somehow knew it would change everything.

CHAPTER FOUR

It was early morning, just barely dawn. All the beds in the house had been full the night before, so my grandma and I were sleeping on the living-room floor together. We were dead to the world when the glimmering red-and-blue lights came streaking through the front window. They danced over the ceiling in a circle, seeping through the lids of our closed eyes, and yanking us up out of our dreams.

I blinked and rubbed my eyes, groggy and confused, but only for a moment. Then my stomach twisted in fear. Those shimmering colored lights chasing each other through the air would have been almost beautiful if I didn't know exactly what they meant.

"David!" my grandma yelled. "Go!"

My fourteen-year-old brother came charging down from his bedroom, taking the stairs three at a time, and was out the back door a split second before the cops exploded into the house, guns drawn and shouting for everyone to "Get down! Get down!"

Our dog Tummy leapt up, barking wildly, and I fell on top of her, holding her flat to the ground as she whimpered and squirmed. I begged her to be silent, terrified that they'd shoot her if she didn't shut up, but the police just streamed past us, filling the house, kicking open doors and waking everyone up in the kind of way that made for nightmares for weeks and weeks after it was all over. There was shouting and screaming and I could hear Washika cry out in one long, inconsolable wail.

They moved from room to room, but our place was small and it didn't take them long to see the back door hanging wide open and figure out where David had gone. Pointing and shouting, they poured out into the grassy alley that ran behind our house and disappeared into the dawn.

This wasn't the first time this had happened. I knew there was almost no chance David was making it out of the alley without getting caught. The cops weren't dumb; no matter which way he ran, they'd already have someone standing there waiting for him on either end. He'd only put off the inevitable finale to this drama by a few moments. If we were lucky, he'd just be grabbed and cuffed, booked, and sent to juvie. If we weren't lucky, the police would make him pay for their efforts, beating him for having the audacity to run. The more they had to chase him, the more he had to pay; so for his sake, I hoped they caught him quick.

Back in the house my mom called down the stairs, "They gone?" and when my grandma gave her the all clear, she came down carrying the still-crying baby in her arms, the rest of my three siblings trailing her in their pajamas, eyes wide, the wash of shock and fear still on their faces. No matter how many times those cops came busting through our door, we were never going to get used to waking up that way.

Tummy whined and licked at my hands, which were still clutched tight around her, holding her in place. I put my face down against the top of her head, gulping in her sharp doggy smell, taking comfort where I could.

"Think they'll catch him?" asked Bee.

"Maybe not this time?" said seven-year-old Gerb. There was a trembling note of hope in his voice.

"Maybe not," agreed my grandma, trying not to extinguish Gerb's optimism. "That boy is fast."

We all nodded in agreement, but deep down we knew it didn't matter how quick David was. There'd be cops wherever he ended up, just waiting to grab him as he ran right into their hands.

"Six of them this time," said Kareema. "I counted."

My mother shook her head and sniffed. "Sending in a whole squad. You'd think they'd have better things to do. He's just a damn child."

We were all quiet for a moment. We knew why they were chasing him. Child or not, David had been dealing drugs on the street corner for months now. As desperately as Lezlie and my mother had tried to keep him out, he was firmly caught up in the life. He certainly wasn't the only kid doing it, but he still lived at home and so he was easy to find. They'd started to pull him in on the regular.

"Well," said my grandma, breaking the silence, "better take y'all asses back to sleep. There's still a few hours before school. We'll track down your brother later on." She looked over toward the kitchen. "Someone best go shut that back door before Tummy goes running out after him. We don't want that dog getting shot."

Gerb, who loved Tummy just as much as I did, went scurrying over to shut the door and then followed the others as they trooped back upstairs.

"Bee?" I asked.

My brother stuck his head over the railing with a questioning look.

"We still gonna ride today?"

Bee smiled his big, warm grin. "For sure, bro."

———

Both of my older brothers were brave. Neither of them seemed to fear anything. They strolled into all sorts of shady situations, hands in their pockets, heads held high, just assuming everything would turn out okay. This was amazing to me, because in our neighborhood, most everything turned out worse than anyone could have imagined.

After we found the barn, Bee learned to channel his fearlessness in a different direction. We'd been in the program for a couple of years when his genius became clear. Lezlie said she'd never seen a kid with such talent. The combination of his cool head and joy for the game made him a brilliant rider and polo player. He was a natural from the moment he first sat in the saddle.

For David, his bravery was more of a curse. He was the child my mother worried about most. Ever since he was little, he'd insisted on doing things his own way; and if he was told that his way was wrong or dangerous, that would only make him want to do it more. If he was not allowed to do what he wanted, he'd just up and leave. And I don't mean walking

down the street with a sandwich in his hand and then returning home by dinner. I'm talking about full-on disappearing,
sometimes for days at a time, to a secret place that no one
could ever find.

David had some natural ability on a horse, but he refused
to put in the time. He'd only ever really been half-in at Work
to Ride. He was twelve when he started riding, and in our
neighborhood, that was plenty grown up. By the time he
was thirteen, he'd dropped out of school and was dealing and
hustling, staying away from home for days on end. By the
time he was fourteen, he was arrested for the first time.

I remember when he went away. We couldn't visit him in
juvenile detention, but we'd line up by the phone every week,
taking turns talking to him, telling him about everything
that was going on in the neighborhood and at the barn. The
first time I talked to him, I thought he might sound different; I thought he'd be sad to be away from us, homesick and
lost, but he sounded fine. It was still the exact same David:
calm, detached, not scared a bit. Instead of being comforted
by the fact that he seemed okay, it chilled me to the bone. He
was impervious. Even jail couldn't seem to crack that wall.

Ever since I was little, I'd trailed after him and Bee any
chance I got. I forced myself into their games, I was their
shadow on the street and at the schoolyard, and if they didn't
let me tag along, I would open up my mouth and cry so long
and hard that my mother would get annoyed and insist they
give me what I wanted.

Bee was a softer touch. We were closer in age, and had
overlapped in primary and middle school. He didn't mind me
being around. But David didn't have time for me. He was so
much older than me, preoccupied with other things, and I

was little and useless and in his way. He was always shaking me off, leaving me behind. So we were never really tight, but that didn't stop the constant worry I felt about what might happen to him. David was growing up, turning into a man, and when I thought about what generally happened to the men in our neighborhood, my stomach hurt. Even as a little kid, I recognized that David's fearlessness was drifting closer and closer to recklessness and that terrified me.

Lezlie did what she could for everyone at Work to Ride, but for whatever reason, she seemed to care the most about us Rosser kids. Maybe it was because our mother was the youngest parent in the program and the least involved at the barn. She was more than happy to step back and trust Lezlie with our care, and Lezlie seemed content to move into that parental vacuum, sometimes even mothering our mother a bit. Maybe it was our talent. We all had a deep and obvious connection to the horses. We all could ride. David had great potential, Bee was extraordinary, and I was getting stronger. Even Gerb had started hanging around the barn at that point. Maybe it was simply because we showed up, day after day, and did the work. Not all the kids in the program did that. But whatever it was, Lezlie loved us as family and that meant that she worried over David as much as the rest of us did.

The first time David came back from juvenile detention, Lezlie did everything she could to make sure he stayed out. She opened up her home to him and he moved in with her. She invited him back into the program and said that as long as he went back to school and got decent grades, he could stay with her and the horses. She tried to keep a grip on him, but the tighter she held on, the more he struggled to get away. Lezlie would punish him whenever he'd step over the line. If he didn't show up at the barn or at school, if he got bad grades or was caught hanging out with people he was supposed to avoid, she'd take away the horses. He was allowed to be at the barn, but he couldn't ride or participate, and that only gave David an excuse to run right back to the streets. He loved the barn, he loved the horses, and he even loved Lezlie, but he loathed an ultimatum. He never could stand being told what to do. It was easy for him to slip away. David didn't need the barn and Lezlie like the rest of us did because he already had a home in the streets.

When he went back to jail for a second time, and then came back out a few months later, Lezlie tried a different way. She decided to stop mothering him and treat him like he was grown. She offered him a real job. She told him he couldn't come back to Work to Ride as a student, but that he could come back to the barn to work as a groom, and she'd pay him what she could and give him a place to stay.

He took the job, but I knew the first day I saw him there that it would never last. Bee and I were riding, chasing down the ball in the field across the street, and David was standing there watching us, pitchfork in hand.

I was a better rider than him by then. We both knew it, and for a moment, I felt both mean and proud about it.

You see? I thought. I could feel my lip curl up in disdain. *You see where you could be if you hadn't decided to fuck it all up?*

I started to show off, spurring Buck into a canter and swooping in to steal the ball from Bee. Bee laughed and shouted. I whooped in response, riding playful circles around my brother. And then I turned back and glanced at David. His face was blank, but I imagined I could see something that looked like regret in his eyes.

I was immediately flooded with shame.

I desperately wanted him to stay. I wanted him to take this chance and keep this job and be safe. I wanted our family to stick together.

But then he turned away and trudged back to the barn, and I knew in my gut that it was only a matter of time. There was nothing for him at the barn anymore. He was sweeping floors and shoveling shit, doing whatever Lezlie asked him to. He couldn't ride or play polo. He couldn't be part of our team. On the street he would have respect and money and the freedom to do what he liked, when he liked. He wouldn't have to answer to anyone.

He was back in jail within two months.

After that, he never came back to the barn, and in a lot of ways he never came back to our family. He turned his back and walked away from us all. There was a crack in my world when he quit. Before then, in my mind, we'd all been safe as long as we had Lezlie, the horses, and the barn. But when David pushed all that aside, a piece of our family—the oldest child, my biggest brother—drifted into a dark and dangerous place. Something that had always felt whole was suddenly broken, and I wasn't sure if it could be fixed again.

CHAPTER FIVE

Man, line, ball! Man, line, ball, Kareem!"

Lezlie was loud. So loud that when she yelled at me from across the field, it felt like she was standing right next to me, screaming in my ear. Buck was being ornery that day, trying to shake me off every few minutes or so, but I managed to stay in my saddle and tried to concentrate on what Lezlie was saying.

Man. That meant defense. When you play polo you pick a player on the opposite team and you need to stay with them no matter what. That day, my man was Bee, and he was not an easy guy to defend against.

Line. Every time the ball is hit, an imaginary line between where the player originally hit the ball and its hoped-for destination is created. That line is like the divider on a highway. For safety's sake, it has to be respected. You can't cross over that line too close to another player without risking a foul and the possibility of dangerous collision.

Ball. You only go after the ball after you take care of your man and establish the line. This was a particularly hard rule for me because I was still fairly new on the field and all I really wanted was to score. I didn't want to play defense or pay attention to the line. I didn't really care about playing as a team. I just wanted to hit that ball as hard as I could and prove that I was supposed to be out there with the big kids.

Bee and I were riding side by side. It was one of those rare, amazing moments when I actually felt like I was keeping up with my big brother. Bee had the ball; he was keeping it in his control by giving it small taps as we thundered down toward his goal. Then he hit it a little too hard and it went spinning out in front of us. I dug my heels into Buck's flanks and urged him forward, leaning out toward the ball, lifting my mallet into the air . . .

Lezlie blew her whistle. "FOUL, Kareem! You crossed the line!"

"What the fuck," I whispered under my breath. I let my mallet fall with a disappointed *swoosh* as Bee galloped past me, throwing me a better-luck-next-time-kid smirk over his shoulder. I pulled on Buck's reins to get him to halt. Instead, he decided to throw out his back legs and send me flying to the ground.

Lezlie blew the whistle again. "You okay?" she shouted.

I stayed on the grass, catching my breath, not opening my eyes, but raising my hand in a little wave to let her know I was fine.

"All right, let's stop there. Time for lunch, anyway!"

I slowly picked myself up and bit back the urge to yell at Buck. Instead, I grabbed his reins and gave an unnecessarily hard yank. "Come on," I said as I limped off the field. As usual, Buck happily followed along.

Bee rode up next to me on his big, potbellied horse, Perfect Rhythm. "You almost had it," he said as he grinned down at me.

I frowned and shook my head. "I'm never gonna get it right. I suck."

Bee poked me in the shoulder with his stick. "Naw, you don't suck. You're gonna get it soon enough. I mean, you're my little brother, aren't you?"

I laughed and rolled my eyes as he rode away.

——

"Polo is kind of like hockey," said Bee.

Bee, Gerb, and I were skipping school, lying on the living-room floor, eating potato chips and watching a stack of VHS tapes that we had borrowed from Lezlie. We'd been at it for hours—polo game after polo game. Bee was explaining the rules to Gerb, who had just started riding at the barn.

"Except no ice," continued Bee. "No goalie. Bigger field, and less players."

We watched a player spur his horse down the field, the ball flying ahead of him.

"And the ponies," I added.

"Why do they even call them ponies?" Gerb asked. "They're not ponies. They're horses."

"Tradition," said Bee. "And because polo horses are trained to be super fast and agile like ponies are."

"I don't know how hockey works," said Gerb.

Bee thought for a moment. "Okay, well, you know how to play soccer, right?"

Gerb and I both nodded.

"So, it's sort of like soccer, too. But with more physical contact. You're allowed to ram your horse into the other guy's horse to throw them off the line and you can hook the other guy's stick with your stick. Oh, and instead of playing two halves, we have seven-and-a-half-minute chukkers. Six of them in field polo, and four in arena."

"Chukkers." Gerb giggled. "Rhymes with fuckers. Chucker fucker."

Bee ignored him and nodded at the TV. "Now, there are four players in field polo, but only three in arena polo like we play. Each player has a different set of responsibilities. Number one is all offense—they make most of the goals. Number two is the midfielder—they set up the shots. Number three is usually the captain—they hit the ball the hardest and decide the strategy. Number four is defense, blocking shots. But anyone can make a goal if they want to, and after a foul, anyone on the team can take the penalty shot."

"Which number do you want to be?" asked Gerb.

"Number three," Bee answered without hesitation. "Naw bro, I'm always gonna be the captain on my team."

We turned back to the TV, watching the game.

"Those boys are flying," said Bee. "Everything has to be fast in this game. We ride fast, and when we hit it right, the ball goes even faster—like, one-hundred-miles-per-hour fast."

"Whoa," I said.

"Yeah," echoed Gerb. "Whoa."

"You have to hit that little plastic ball with your mallet through the goal posts. And when you do, your team gets a point. After someone gets a point, we switch goals. Oh shit! Look at that!"

We all gasped as we watched a horse stumble and then fall on the field, taking his rider down with him.

Bee stopped the tape and hit rewind and made us watch it again. I shuddered as the horse rolled over its rider.

"People die playing polo," said Bee. His voice was serious. "People die all the time."

"Did that guy die?" asked Gerb, pointing at the TV.

I shook my head. "Naw, see? He's getting up."

"His horse all right?" asked Gerb. He sounded more worried about the horse than the rider.

Bee put his arm around Gerb's shoulders. "They're both okay, bro. Look, they're taking the pony off the field."

Gerb frowned. "Maybe it's not fair to make the ponies play polo. They can get hurt. What if they don't want to play?"

I shook my head. "Gerb. They're fine. They love playing."

"They do," agreed Bee. "Polo ponies are athletes, too. A player ain't nothing without his horse. You should see Rhythm when I get him on the field. He's so happy. He was born to play."

Gerb bit his lip. "But what if I'm not born to play? What if I fall off and get hurt like that? How we know I'm not gonna suck at polo?"

Bee grinned and stretched out on the floor, resting his head in the crooks of his arms. "Shit, bro, no worries. All us Rosser kids were made to play. That's who we are."

——

Bee wasn't always Bee. Before he started playing polo he was just Jabarr. I liked to think about that sometimes, how my brother was one person before he got on a horse and someone altogether different after.

Since David left the barn I had been getting better and better at riding, and sometimes even keeping up on the polo field, but I had to work my ass off to get there.

For Bee, it just came naturally.

Lezlie had put together a team consisting of eleven-year-old Bee and a couple of the teen boys from the barn and started taking them to the Cowtown Polo Club in New Jersey to play games. Gerb and I came along to help load and unload the ponies and hot-walk in between chukkers.

Cowtown was not your average polo club. It was one of the few clubs I would ever encounter that was middle class and blue collar. The members weren't billionaires and the elite; they were plumbers and teachers and small business owners. Instead of an immaculately groomed polo field, we played on an actual cow pasture. They would corral the cattle off the fields just before a game, but we still had to be careful to avoid the wallows and divots the cows had made, not to mention the fact that there was cow shit everywhere.

Still, it was a big step up from the soccer field across from the barn, and Bee was excited to be playing. The team Bee played on was terrible; the other boys fumbled around the field like the amateurs they were, and they only won a handful of games, but Bee was still a star on the field. He was playing so well that word got around and people started to come to games just to see what this little kid could do. He was still small back then, and sneaky; he would dart in and grab the ball so fast that the other players never saw him coming. Bigger, more prestigious clubs started calling Lezlie when they needed a ringer, asking if he could come play on their teams for a game or two.

And they weren't asking for Jabarr, they were asking for his new name, the Killer Bee.

———

"Reem, I know you didn't take my broom again!" My mom was calling from the kitchen.

I wrenched open the front door and took the steps two at a time. "Sorry! Can't hear you, Mom!" I yelled as I took off running down the street.

Her voice followed me outside. "Boy, you better come back here! KAREEM!"

Laughing, I rounded the corner and found Gerb and Bee waiting for me.

"Cool," said Bee as he reached for the broom. He put his foot against the stick and cracked the head off in one swift motion, throwing the pile of now useless straw into the street. Then he handed me and Gerb two big tree branches we had scavenged from our neighbor's yard. "Okay, now we can play."

We faced each other in the street, making a triangle. Bee slowly lifted up the empty plastic water bottle he'd dug out of the trash, and threw it into the air.

I caught it on my branch and knocked it down the road, and we were off—racing each other, waving our sticks in the air, using the streetlights as goals, driving our neighbors crazy as we yelled and screamed and batted around that water bottle like we were playing the Argentine Open and tied up in our sixth chukker.

There was nothing else we wanted to do. Since we joined the barn, if we couldn't actually be on a horse, we were either talking about polo, watching it on TV, or playing this make-shift version on the street.

I fell and ripped open my knee, Gerb almost got hit by a car, and Bee got cussed out by our neighbor when he knocked the water bottle through their open kitchen window, but we kept playing until long after dark.

Finally we got tired and hungry enough to call it quits. We stashed the branches and stick behind a bunch of garbage cans in the alley and headed out, laughing and talking trash as we made our way home.

Then, as we rounded the corner, we stopped, staring. There was a new memorial up: flowers and balloons, scattered cards and notes, a teddy bear, and a big plastic cross. There was a framed picture of a smiling young man. He looked about twenty. I squinted at the photo. None of us recognized him, but we quieted down as we walked home. We had been raised to be respectful when faced with a fresh death.

—

Everyone else was in bed, but Bee, Gerb, and I were still up, watching another game in the living room, a choppy video of the Heguy brothers winning the Argentine Open in 1986.

It was late summer in Philly and we didn't have air-conditioning; the house was airless and hot. Our mom had turned all the lights out when she went to bed, so the only illumination was the flickering blue light of the TV. We had draped our bodies limply across the floor, sitting up on our elbows and fanning ourselves with paper plates from the pizza we'd eaten earlier, sweating through our shorts and T-shirts.

"Whoa," said Gerb as we watched images of the "Heguy Express" rocketing down the field. "You said they're brothers?"

"Yup," said Bee. "Their father and uncles won the Open

back in their day, too. And now these guys have kids who are also ten-goal players. It's a family dynasty."

"It's kind of crazy," I said. "How'd they all get so good?"

"Because in Argentina, the kids are put on ponies before they can walk," answered Bee. "They give babies tiny polo sticks instead of rattles. They eat, drink, and breathe polo from the time they're born."

I imagined this for a moment—a little baby Washika's size, sitting on a pony and holding a shrunken mallet. I decided right then and there that if I ever had kids, I would do exactly the same.

We watched the brothers score goal after goal, playing together like a machine, each player making it possible for his brothers to perform at their highest abilities.

"You know," said Bee, his voice sounding low and dreamy. "That could be us."

I turned to him, surprised. "How?" I demanded.

"Yeah, how?" asked Gerb.

Bee didn't take his eyes off the screen. "We could have a family team. I'm good, and you're getting better, Kareem, and Gerb already knows what he's doing on a horse. If we worked real, real hard, I don't see why we couldn't do what these guys did."

I blinked. "You really think so?"

Bee nodded. "Yeah. I do. I bet we could get sponsored, too. Get a patron. They'd pay for us to play."

"Really?" said Gerb.

Bee finally looked away from the television and turned toward us. His eyes were bright with excitement. "We could have a farm, too. We know about horses, right? Lez already taught us everything we need. We could breed and train and sell our polo ponies. You know how much a good polo pony goes for?"

I shook my head mutely.

"Like fifty thousand dollars."

I felt my eyes go wide. "For one horse?" I said.

"The best ones go for even more. Like a quarter of a million."

"Shit," said Gerb. "That's crazy!"

"What about Mom and the girls?" I asked. "Could they live there, too?"

"And David?" added Gerb. "I mean, when he gets out of juvie?"

"Why not?" said Bee. "Look at these guys." He gestured at the TV. "I bet they had a farm. I bet they all practiced and played together every day. That could be us, too. In fact—" he sat up straighter, "—it's going to be us. I've decided."

I felt a knot of longing in my chest expand so big I could barely breathe. I could see it. I could see the quiet farm out in the country. I could see the big white house with green shutters, and the red stables and our ponies. I could see the family working together, us kids taking care of the horses while Mom sat on the front porch watching and drinking iced tea. We'd have our own polo field, and I could see all of us brothers playing, winning games, getting trophies. No guns. No drugs. No jail. No police knocking down our doors. Just us, somewhere green and safe and peaceful.

Family team, I thought, and the words felt exactly right.

———

"Where is your brother?"

Lezlie was pissed, and I guess she had every right to be. We had a game in less than an hour and Bee was already forty-five minutes late. Even if we left right at that moment, we'd barely make it for the tip-off.

I shrugged. I truly didn't know exactly where he was, but I had a strong hunch that I wasn't about to share with Lezlie.

Bee had been skipping school again. Not just a class here and there, but days, and even weeks, at a time. Sometimes Gerb and I skipped with him and we'd all hang out, but some days, I didn't know where Bee went. He just disappeared.

It made me sick to my stomach with worry when he was gone. There were nights when he didn't come home, either. I'd lie awake in bed, thinking that if I wished it hard enough, I'd hear the front door open and Bee come clomping up the stairs.

Lezlie always knew when he missed school. Bee's guidance counselor had started calling Lezlie instead of our mom because she knew that at least there would be consequences at the barn. So Bee had started to avoid the barn because he didn't want to have to look Lezlie in the eye and explain himself. He'd skipped school every day last week. I was pretty sure he wasn't showing up for this game because he knew that Lezlie would be waiting to chew him out.

When Bee first started riding—before polo, even—his natural seat was so good that Lezlie would take him to shows and sign him up to compete in levels way above his skill set. He'd ride out there and make all sorts of mistakes, but he looked so pretty on his pony that he almost always came away with the blue ribbon anyway. The judges just couldn't resist him. They knew a natural when they saw one. On the field, it was the same. He was born to it. Practice or not, everything just came easy to Bee. He was only becoming a more undeniable player with every passing game. When he was out there riding Rhythm, he could score four goals a chukker as simple as shrugging his shoulders. I knew he loved the horses, loved polo, loved the barn, but I also knew that playing at all these new polo clubs had changed things for him. Suddenly, he was seeing all we couldn't have: the strings of professional ponies, the gear, and the money. And the acceptance. They may have been calling him in as a ringer, but he was still the only Black face on the field. Despite all his talent, he was not part of their world.

Plus there was the money, or rather, the lack of money. Things were no easier at home financially. Our mother was still struggling. Even the barn was struggling. There were days when Lezlie would cancel riding because she didn't have enough feed for the horses, and she would send us out into the street with homemade cardboard signs soliciting donations for the program. No part of this was easy.

My stomach twisted in knots as it got later and later and I watched Lezlie get more and more upset, the look on her face moving between anger and worry and sadness. Finally, she looked at her watch and rubbed the space between her eyes. "We'll have to forfeit." She shook her head as she walked toward her office to make the call. "This is not happening again," she said to no one in particular. "Not this time."

———

"But how long will you be gone?" I whispered to Bee.

We were lying side by side in bed. Bee had just told me that Lezlie and our mother were sending him to live on a three-hundred-acre polo farm in Fort Worth, Texas. That a friend of Lezlie's, a woman named Cissy who managed the farm, had agreed to take him in.

I felt him shrug in the darkness. "I don't know. As long as this lady wants me, I guess."

"But what does that mean? Like, years?"

He shrugged again. "I guess so. Maybe."

I was quiet for a moment, trying to process the indeterminate parameters of his absence.

"Do you want to go?"

He hesitated. Slow to answer. I could practically hear him thinking in the dark. "Yeah," he finally said. "I guess I do."

"But, Bee—"

"I'll be able to play every day, Reem. And not on some dumb soccer field. They have three professional polo fields, an indoor arena, hundreds of perfectly trained ponies. I'll meet real players. I'll get the training I need."

"But you don't even know this person."

He sighed. "I met her once. She seemed okay for a white lady. Lezlie says she's nice."

"Texas is so far away." We'd never been farther than New Jersey.

"It is," he agreed.

I hesitated. "Do you . . . do you think you'll ever come back?"

I felt him shift toward me. "To live?" he said. "I don't know."

But what about me and Gerb? What about the family team?

I couldn't bring myself to say it out loud, but it was like he heard me anyway.

His shoulder touched mine. "Yo, listen to me. The thing is, if I get really good, it will open the door for all of us."

I swallowed hard. I was glad it was too dark for him to see my face.

"I'll call a lot," he said. "And maybe you can come down and visit me sometime. There's that summer camp. We can see each other then."

"Yeah," I said, trying to keep my voice steady. "I guess that could be cool."

Bee yawned. "Okay, I'm tired. Go to sleep, little man. This will be fine. You'll see."

He turned his back to me. After a moment, I could hear his breathing slow down as he let go and slipped away into sleep. All my siblings were dreaming in that room, a small concert of snores and sighs, groans and murmurs.

I kept my eyes open, though, staring into the dark.

CHAPTER SIX

The barn felt different without Bee. Hollow. Empty.

Gerb was there, of course, but Gerb was a little kid, still learning to ride, and besides, he had friends his own age at the barn. He'd always been independent. It didn't feel like he needed me much back then.

My twin sister, Kareema, joined the barn after Bee left. You hear things about twins—how they have this magical connection—but that had never exactly been the case for Kareema and me. We definitely had certain things in common, mainly the fact that we were both overly cautious in a family full of daredevils, but we orbited each other more than we connected. She had her friends and, up until that moment, I'd had my brothers. She never really wanted to tag along with us when we were out running wild.

Kareema was shy and gentle. She was happy at the barn. Like the rest of us, she loved animals and she especially loved the horses. She even played a polo game or two once in a while, but she didn't have that killer instinct.

"That's okay. No, thank you," she'd mostly say whenever someone asked her if she wanted to play. She sounded so sweet, but there was something about the way she said no that made it clear there was no point in asking her again.

Kareema was given an older black thoroughbred mare named Arquetta to take care of, and she would spend hours just grooming and braiding the horse's mane and tail. When Arquetta was done up to her liking, and Kareema finally climbed up to ride, she had good form but was timid. She didn't like speed and she took no chances. Like I had been with Angel, Kareema was a one-horse rider. She refused to ride anyone but Arquetta. But unlike me, Lezlie never got the chance to force Kareema onto another horse.

There were other girls at the barn, jumpers and dressage riders; they moved in a horsey pack. It took Kareema no time at all to fit in with them. Even if I wanted to spend more time with my sister, those girls were not interested in including a scrawny ten-year-old boy in their equine clique.

I was a little lost without Bee, and I was a little jealous of Gerb and Kareema. Losing Bee didn't seem to hit them the same way it hit me. They seemed to find it so easy to make friends and get on with things, but I was adrift.

Every week I would wait for the chance to talk to my big brother, looking forward to his weekly call, thinking about all the stuff I needed to catch him up on, dying to hear about everything he was seeing and learning. But when we finally got on the phone, Bee didn't sound quite like Bee. He seemed like a slightly different person who was living in a world I couldn't even begin to imagine. Even his voice changed, a

Texas twang becoming more pronounced with every passing week.

I started to cling to Lezlie, following her around the barn like an aimless puppy, sitting in her lap whenever she sat down, grabbing her arm and hanging off her whenever she stood up, keeping her in my line of sight at all times. She was tolerant of my neediness. Maybe she missed Bee and David, too. Or maybe she just saw how lost I was and knew I needed the extra love.

The one bright spot was polo. Now that Bee was gone, Lezlie had moved me up and given me his place on the team that he'd left behind. Without Bee, the team was truly beyond horrible; we never won, we rarely even scored, but it still gave me some relief. As hopeless as we were, I still got to feel that momentary, visceral thrill when we rode onto the Cowtown field, carefully avoiding the cow patties strewn throughout the grass, and turned to face the applauding crowd. And I still felt fiercely determined to get better and learn. If Bee ever returned, I needed to be ready to play alongside him.

So when a bright, fearless twelve-year-old girl named Mecca Harris rode up to the barn one day flanked by a small herd of Black Cowboys, gave us all an ear-to-ear grin, and announced she wanted to join Work to Ride and earn a place on our polo team, I probably should have been worried or threatened. But instead, from the moment I first saw her, I was completely in her thrall.

—

I don't know why Mecca chose me. There were lots of kids at the barn—girls and boys, tougher, less anxious people than me, better riders, braver souls, but Mecca didn't seem to care. The very first morning she was at the barn, she marched right up to me and Buck and began asking questions.

"What's your name? How old are you? How long have you been riding? What's your favorite thing about horses? Do you play polo? How good are you? What's Lezlie like? Is this your horse? What's his name? Is he a good horse? Can I ride him sometime?"

I just stood there, slack jawed. It had been so long since anyone had paid any real attention to me, I barely knew how to answer.

Mecca shook her head impatiently at my hesitation and turned to walk away. I opened my mouth, wanting her to come back, but before I could say anything, she looked over her shoulder and flashed me her unforgettable smile. "C'mon, what are you waiting for?" she said. "Let's ride. We out."

After one day of riding with Mecca, I knew I'd lose my place on the team. Like Bee, Mecca was a killer, afraid of nothing, thrilled by speed, and a complete natural on the field. She'd never played polo before, but she casually picked up that mallet, swung herself up into the saddle, and took off like a ten-goal pro. And like Bee, when I watched her play, she made me a better rider, because if she could do something, I wouldn't rest until I learned to do it, too.

From that day forward, we were inseparable. I was her shadow; if you saw Mecca, you saw me. My days were suddenly joyful in a way they had never been before. Mecca didn't seem to notice our age difference, or care about the fact that I was a skinny little boy whose head barely reached her shoulders; and it didn't matter to me that she was stronger, more skilled, and could kick my ass on and off the field.

Before Mecca, I'd had my brothers, but I'd never really had a best friend.

We were each assigned a horse to care for when we joined the club, and Mecca had one of the best ones in the stable: Buddha, a black Argentine thoroughbred mare. Someone must have named her as a joke, because she was anything but Zen. She was high energy, always ready to run, fit and beautiful, but gentle enough so that any kid could ride her. She taught dozens of children over the years, but only if Mecca wasn't around. Because if Mecca was in the barn, no one else was allowed to touch her pony. She loved that animal with all of her heart and soul, and that pony loved her right back. They were the same: spirited and fun loving and strong and beautiful. They both seemed a little reckless on the outside, but scratch the surface and there was nothing but sweetness underneath. I loved to ride Buck alongside Mecca and Buddha. There was something about that mare that calmed down my wild horse, made him forget that his favorite thing was shaking me off his back like I was a tick and he was the dog. When he was running with Buddha, Buck would drop his bad-boy act and simply do his best to keep up.

——

"Psst!"

I stopped brushing Buck and looked around. I could hear someone, but couldn't see them.

"Psst! Reem!"

It had to be Mecca. I spun around. Still nothing.

"Yo, dummy! Look the fuck up here!"

I smiled as I finally spotted her waving at me from up in the hayloft. "You better hope that Lez doesn't hear you talking that way. You know she'll wash your mouth out with soap."

Mecca rolled her eyes. "Big fucking deal. My mouth always tastes like soap these days. Come up here when you're done with Buck."

The hayloft was a gallery that was open on one side and ran the full length of the barn. We used it for all sorts of things: to hide from Lezlie when we were in trouble, to stash treats we didn't want to share with the whole club, to eat our lunch, our legs dangling in the air, looking down at the horses below.

"I've got an idea," whispered Mecca after I climbed up the stairs. "What time do you think Lez is going to peace out?"

"Around seven, usually." I said.

"And what time is it now?"

I shrugged. "About six thirty?"

Mecca grinned and then leaned out over the loft. "Hey there, Lez!" she shouted. "Me and Kareem are going on home now! See you tomorrow!"

"Stop shouting!" yelled Lezlie from her office. "You're going to scare the horses! Have a good night, you two! Nice riding today!"

Mecca grabbed my sleeve and pulled me toward the stairs. I looked at her, confused. She dug her elbow into my side. "Tell her goodnight and thank you," she hissed as we tromped down the stairs.

"Goodnight, Lez!" I parroted as we left the barn. "Thank you!"

We ran all the way back to The Bottom, finally stopping when we got to Mecca's house. Her mom was home for once. Mecca's mom was like my mom, working all the time.

"Hey, Mama," said Mecca as she opened up the fridge and began hauling out whatever she could find: string cheese and apples and cans of pop, stuffing them into her pockets until they were full and then handing over more food to stuff into mine. "I'm going to spend the night at Kareem's tonight, okay?"

I wrinkled my nose. "You are?" I whispered. We never spent the night at my house. We always stayed at hers. More room, fewer kids.

She rolled her eyes at me and blew out an exasperated breath. "Okay, Mama?"

"Sure, honey," said Mecca's mother. She sounded like she was only half listening.

Mecca was in the pantry now, filling a paper bag with packages of potato chips and Oreos.

"Bye, Mama!" Mecca didn't wait for her mother to answer before slamming the door behind us and heading back out into the street.

"Why are we bringing all that junk to my house?" I asked. "I got food, you know."

Mecca socked me in the shoulder. "God, quit acting so dumb!" she said.

"Ow! Why?" I yelped. Mecca punched hard.

"We're not going to your house, dummy. We're going back to the barn!"

———

The barn was different after hours, dark and shadowy. We didn't want to attract any notice, so we kept the lights off and grabbed one of the emergency flashlights from Lezlie's office. Mecca led the way, stopping at each stall so we could speak to every horse in turn, scratching their noses and rubbing their necks, whispering their names.

"We really going to spend the whole night?" I said as we climbed up into the hayloft.

Mecca turned back to look at me and her dark eyes gleamed with glee. "The whole night," she breathed. "We just have to get up early enough to get out of here before Lezlie shows up in the morning. Think we can do that?"

I nodded solemnly. "Sure," I said. I was so excited, I was certain I wouldn't close my eyes at all.

Mecca turned over her paper bag and we emptied our pockets, making a small pile of junk food on the floor of the loft.

I reached for a box of cookies but Mecca shook her head. "Help me first," she said as she grabbed a hay bale and started dragging it across the floor.

We spent the next hour building the perfect fort, a snug little hay-and-straw igloo that we could squeeze into side by side, lying on our stomachs and kicking up our heels while we ate our picnic. After dinner, we stuffed our garbage back into the paper bag, and then turned over, eyes now on the dark ceiling of our fort. We lay there shoulder to shoulder, listening to the soft, comforting sounds of the horses as they shifted around in their stalls, smelling the hay and manure, the warm, dusty scent that rose up from the bodies of the horses, and whisper-arguing over which horse was better, who could ride harder, who loved the ponies more.

Eventually our whispers slowed down and then stopped, and we drifted off to sleep, tucked away like a couple of old barn cats bedded down in the straw. Two little kids in the middle of a dark Philly night. We were alone in the stables, but we weren't scared at all. We were certain we had never been safer. The barn was the best place we knew.

—

"Kareem! Kareem! Wake up!"

My eyes popped open and I saw Mecca's face looming over me. I struggled for a moment, trying to remember where we were, but then I saw a whole thatch of straw caught in Mecca's hair.

I laughed. "You look like a scarecrow."

"We gotta go!" she hissed. "Lez will be here anytime now!"

"Oh shit!" I jumped up, terrified by the thought of being caught, and we ran, clattering down the stairs, into the pale morning light.

As we raced through the barn, every pony in that place watched us, shaking their manes and stomping the ground like they knew we weren't supposed to be there. We laughed as we slipped out of the stables, our hearts racing as we imagined every car that drove by to have Lezlie at the wheel. Finally we really did see Lezlie's old junker of a car turn the corner.

"Oh shit!" I yelped. "Oh no!"

"Come on!" Mecca grabbed me by the hand and pulled me off the path.

We went flying through the woods. We ran until we were out of the park and back up into our neighborhood. We didn't slow down until we were safe in my house and flopped down on the living-room floor.

Everyone else in my house was asleep upstairs. Mecca and I were flat on our backs, panting and sweating and still holding hands. We looked at each other, grinning idiotically. I reached over with my other hand, tugged a straw out of her hair, and showed it to her. She laughed, and then did the same to me.

"Wanna do it again tonight?" she whispered, squeezing my fingers so hard it almost hurt.

I nodded and squeezed back. I thought I'd never seen a face I liked looking at more.

CHAPTER SEVEN

Y ou think if the plane crashed and we fell down on top of one, it could hold us up?" I asked Mecca.

She laughed, craning her neck so she could see out my little window. "Clouds are just vapor, Reem. They're not holding up anything. Don't you remember that from science class?"

I shook my head. "Must have skipped that day."

I rested my forehead against the airplane window and stared out at the sky some more, equally unsettled and excited by how strange it looked. Big, white, billowy clouds below, bright blue air all around, and a blurry patchwork of brown and gray land down there at the very bottom.

It was the first time either of us had flown. We were going to polo camp in Fort Worth, Texas.

I looked back down at the clouds. "Are you sure that they're just vapor? Cuz—"

"You think he'll like me okay?" interrupted Mecca.

I turned back toward her, wrinkling my nose. "Who?" I asked.

"Bee." She didn't meet my eyes, like she was embarrassed to have asked.

"Why wouldn't he?"

She shrugged. "I don't know. It's silly, I guess."

I shook my head at her strangeness. "I'm sure he'll like you just fine."

She nodded. "I saw him play once, you know."

"You saw Bee play?"

"Yeah. I saw him play at a game in New Jersey. Just before he left. He was so good. He was riding so fast. Y'all went into overtime and had to play sudden death." Her eyes looked almost dreamy.

"Yeah, I remember that game," I said. "Bee won it just before the horn."

Mecca nodded again. "That's when I decided to quit the Black Cowboys and join the barn. I wanted to ride like that, too."

I shrugged. "I mean, we all want to ride like Bee does."

She bit down on her thumbnail. "I just hope he's cool with me."

—

"You lost your place on the team to a girl? You mad or naw?"

Bee and I were watching Mecca lead a little white mare into the stables and attach her to the cross ties at the other end of the barn.

I shot a look at my brother, kind of pleased that he was giving me shit—because teasing each other was what we did—but still feeling a little flustered.

It had been almost a year since I last saw him, and Bee had changed in all sorts of ways. He was still small for his age, but he was taller, more muscular, and his voice was deeper, not to mention that Texas accent that kept creeping in. He dressed different. He looked pure country now; no more baggy pants and oversized T-shirts. He was wearing a plaid button-down shirt tucked into a pair of tight-fitting Wranglers. Actual shit-kicking cowboy boots.

I shrugged. "She's really dope, bro," I said. "Just watch."

Bee poked me in the side. "What? Is she your girlfriend or something?"

I blushed and shook my head violently. "Naw, man. It's not like that. Mecca's just my friend. My best friend."

Bee laughed. "Okay. Whatever you say, Reem. Go get your pony ready. Let's play a couple of chukkers."

—

We were there for a week. It was a summer camp run by the Polo Training Foundation. Bee was a junior counselor and Mecca and I had been given full scholarships to come and ride. There were a bunch of other kids there with us, all different ages, from a lot of different places, but the three of us were the only Black folk on the farm.

I couldn't believe that Bee actually got to live in this place. The stables were nicer than any house I'd ever set foot in. Three hundred acres, four regulation-size polo fields, an indoor arena, and dozens of the fanciest ponies I had ever seen. Not to mention an Olympic-size swimming pool complete with a built-in hot tub that Mecca and I made immediate plans to sneak into after dark. Bee lived in the caretaker's house with Cissy and her family, right on the property. He could just walk out the door, saddle up a horse, and play every day, and he had some of the best players out there showing him how it was done.

This was the first time I truly understood that there was a side to the polo world that wasn't just a bunch of kids fooling around on the field. No one was playing this game in the middle of cow shit. I thought about how different this place was from Work to Ride. We didn't have an indoor. We barely had a decent field. Once it snowed, we couldn't even get on a horse until spring thaw. Bee's everyday pony was a little paint named Rosie who was so fine that she made Buck, and even Buddha, look like we'd pulled them out of the glue factory in comparison.

I was wide eyed when Bee showed us around, but with every fancy detail he pointed out, I got a little sadder. I couldn't see a reason why my brother would ever leave this place. I was pretty sure he'd never come home again.

—

We were watching Mecca race across the grass with one of the adult pros who were there to teach us.

"Okay, yeah, you were right. She can play, bro. You gonna be riding the bench forever."

I hit Bee in the arm as hard as I could.

He hit me back. "Okay, okay, chill out," he said.

Mecca leaned over and made a spectacular steal.

Bee whistled. "Oh shit! Your *best friend* is a goddamned monster on the field."

I grinned. "I told you. Lezlie says she'll be as good as you if she keeps working at it."

Bee snorted. "Calm down, son. She good, but you ain't even really seen me play yet. Let's not go fuckin' overboard."

—

Bee was right. He wasn't only different off the field. When I watched him play for the first time, I realized that he was probably a hundred times better on horseback than he'd been the last time I'd seen him ride. He was thirteen years old, but he looked like an actual pro, dressed in white jeans and a jersey, speeding across the grass, sending that ball spinning off into the distance. Mecca and I watched him with our mouths hanging open as he darted and swerved, making the tightest turns and the most clever steals. We'd never seen anyone play like Bee could.

And we weren't the only ones who thought so. Other counselors told me that people in the polo world were talking about him like crazy. He'd started to get a national reputation for his skill, climbing up the rankings and winning games left and right. People were offering all sorts of things. There was talk of him going to Argentina for a year, getting the chance to train with the pros down there. There were colleges that had polo teams and they were already sending scouts out to watch him play.

I was both jealous and wildly impressed. By the second day, I had shaken off the awkwardness I'd initially felt and I started to ask a million questions. It was like old times; I followed my big brother wherever he went, desperate to learn anything he could teach me. The only difference was that now I had Mecca by my side, just as eager to learn. I couldn't believe that we only had a week to absorb everything Bee knew.

———

"You're really good," said Mecca bluntly as we sat at the table and ate our dinner. "You're way better than the last time I saw you play, and you were already good then. I didn't know a kid could play like you can."

Bee laughed. "Um, thanks, I guess."

I'd been concentrating hard on the pile of fried chicken I had on my plate—even the food was better here—but I looked up at them and hastily swallowed. "Mecca saw you play at Cowtown," I said.

Bee smiled and shook his head. "Hard to imagine playing on that old field again."

"It's better than the soccer field, at least," said Mecca.

Bee rolled his eyes. "True that."

I took a bite of cornbread. "We're gonna have a family team someday," I told Mecca with my mouth full. "Me, Gerb, and Bee will be the captain."

Mecca raised her eyebrows at us. "You'll need a fourth if you want to play polo on the grass."

I nodded. "Okay. You can be the fourth."

Bee laughed again. "Oh yeah? She can?"

"Sure," I said. "You know anyone better?"

Bee looked at her for a long second, considering. Then he shrugged. "Fair enough." He picked up his fork. "I guess she's in. She can be our fourth."

Mecca grinned. "But what if I want to be the captain?"

Bee whistled. "Okay, calm down—" he started to say.

"Let's not go fuckin' overboard," I finished up, doing my

best Texas accent. Then I picked up another drumstick and bit down, smiling as Mecca laughed and threw her balled up napkin across the table, somehow managing to hit us both.

—

Saying goodbye to camp was hard. A week wasn't a long time but the days were packed so full, it felt like we'd been there much longer. I knew I would miss the endless green fields and the well-trained ponies. I would miss having a comfortable bed to myself in the bunkhouse. I would even miss the grits and the redeye gravy we ate every morning. But all that was nothing compared to how I felt leaving my big brother behind once again. I'd seen where he was living now, and I couldn't imagine him ever wanting to come back to stay on Viola Street.

"You guys will come back next summer," said Bee as he walked us to the bus that was taking us back to the airport. "And maybe I can come up for Christmas. Cissy said she thinks it would be a good idea if I went back home to visit sometime soon." He rolled his eyes. "I think she wants me to remember just how good I have it here."

I nodded, trying to play it cool. "Well, better not wear those Wranglers if you do."

Mecca nodded solemnly in agreement. "You gonna have the shit kicked out of you if you show up looking like that, country boy."

"Get the fuck out of my face," said Bee as he slung an arm around each of our necks and squeezed.

—

Back on the plane, I tried to hold back the tears as we taxied up the runway.

"You okay?" asked Mecca.

I quickly turned my head away from her, trying to hide my face.

She took my hand. "Don't worry. We'll see him soon enough."

I nodded, still looking away. I wanted to answer, but I was afraid that if I opened my mouth, I'd just sob.

"And don't forget," Mecca said. "We're gonna have the family team."

I looked at her and slowly nodded. "That's true," I said, sniffing.

Mecca gave me a twisted little smile. "I'm sad, too," she admitted, and she didn't let go of my hand until we were back in the air and flying again.

—

"I'm done for the night, Reem. You want to come?" Mecca halted her horse at the gate. "Daryl won some money so Mom says he's bringing home Chinese. We're going to celebrate."

"Naw," I said, keeping my horse at a steady trot. "Buck still needs to run. You go on ahead. I'll holla at you tomorrow."

"Cool," called Mecca cheerfully as she wheeled Buddha around and headed off toward the barn. "I'll see you then, bro!"

"Bye!" I said carelessly as I kicked Buck into a canter. I didn't want to miss my chance to stay a little later and try to catch up with Mecca's superior riding skills.

I pushed Buck that night, determined to make the most of my time. I rode alone in the ring, switching between a trot and a canter until it was cold and almost dark and every muscle in my body started to ache. Ever since we'd returned from Texas,

I had been determined to become a better horseman. I wanted to earn my place on our family team.

Finally, when the sun was almost down, I slowed my horse to a walk and took him around the ring a last few times, cooling him off. Exhausted, I dismounted and led him back into the barn.

Lezlie was still in her office; the warm yellow light from her desk lamp spilled out into the stables, but most everyone else had gone home for the night.

I tied up Buck, stripped him of his saddle, and picked up my tack box. I always liked to groom. It was a tangible thing; it gave me peace. In my head, I recited the parts of my pony as I rubbed the grooming mitt over his body, just like Bee had taught me so long ago: *muzzle, forehead, poll, crest, withers* . . . And when I reached the end, and there was nothing more to do, I put him away, topped up his water, gave him his feed, put up my tack, said goodbye to Lezlie, and walked home as the darkness fell.

——

In the meantime, back in The Bottom, Mecca, my best friend, my soul mate, the person I loved most in the world, was already gone.

CHAPTER EIGHT

This is what we know: He interrupted them while they were eating dinner. The Chinese food was still on the table, half eaten, a box of rice spilled on its side.

He told them to go down into the basement, showing them his gun so that they knew there was no other choice. He followed behind as he marched them down the stairs.

He lined them up and shot them, one by one, execution style. We know the order of death because of the way the bodies fell: first Mecca's stepdad Daryl, then her mother Sheila, and finally, Mecca. A bullet to the head, each body crumpling against the next.

He left them down there, went back upstairs, and ransacked their house. Looking for something. Then he let himself out their back door and ran into the night.

This is what we don't know: His name. His age. If he knew Mecca's family personally. If he was the least bit sorry for what he did. If he felt anything at all as he looked into the eyes of a child and then violently ended her life.

This is the part that I will never get over: He made Mecca go last. How terrified and sad she must have been. How horribly long those last few seconds between gunshots must have felt to her. How he forced my beautiful, brave, generous fourteen-year-old friend—a girl who had never been afraid of anything—to spend the last moments of her life filled with the worst kind of terror and sorrow.

———

Lezlie usually picked up me, Gerb, and Kareema after school, so when we came outside and I saw a couple of the volunteers from the barn standing there instead, I knew right away something bad had happened. And as soon as I got closer and saw their faces, I knew someone had been killed. I'd seen that look enough times to recognize it, that particular combination of sick and sad and scared.

I understood death. No one grows up where I grew up and doesn't understand what death is. People had died in my neighborhood, on my block, and in my family. There was a homemade cross and a pile of wilted flowers on practically every street corner in my neighborhood. Every other person had a gun or sold drugs or both, and we'd all heard stories about the random bullet gone astray. But I always thought kids who stayed out of the game were safe. We weren't any part of the life—why should we be in any danger? So, the first person I thought of when I saw those volunteers was David. Then I thought, what if it was my mom? Or even Lezlie? It never even occurred to me to worry about Mecca.

If I'd stood there on that sidewalk all day, I never would have guessed it was her.

One of the volunteers knelt down on the sidewalk so he could look us in the eyes as he told us what had happened. When he said Mecca's name, the only thing I remember was a single scream rising up from my guts, unstoppable, like a gush of vomit or blood.

They said Lezlie was waiting for everyone at the barn. That she wanted us all together, in a safe place. Somehow they got us into the car.

On the ride over, Kareema and Gerb were crying, but I went numb and dull. I looked out the window and watched the streets roll by and decided it was all a big mistake.

It was someone else. Mecca is fine. Someone just got the story wrong.

We got to the barn and Lezlie hugged us one by one. When she put her arms around me, I leaned into her, waiting for her to tell me that I was right, that Mecca was waiting for us all in the barn, wondering why everyone was making such a big fucking fuss. When I felt Lezlie shaking, trying to hold back her own tears, I wrenched myself away. I refused to feel anything that made it real.

—

There was a candlelight vigil at Mecca's house that evening; hundreds of people from all over the neighborhood came together, standing shoulder to shoulder, praying and singing and crying. I stood there between my mom and Lezlie, holding a taper in my hands, feeling nothing. Slack and empty and dull. People cried and wailed all around me, but I just stared at Mecca's narrow little row house. Waiting. I was certain that my friend was inside, hiding out, probably watching me through the window, giggling at all our foolishness. I was sure that if I stood there long enough, the front door would open and she would come flying out, laughing and ready to run.

A preacher asked us to bow our heads and pray.

I stepped forward while everyone's eyes were still closed. I blew out my candle and dropped it on the ground. I broke away from my mom and Lez and slipped under the police tape that blocked off Mecca's porch. I walked toward the window, absolutely sure I was going to come face-to-face with my friend's sweet, mischievous smile.

But the window was empty. There was no Mecca. And as I looked into that house that I knew as well as my own, I felt the world tilt under me. Nothing was in its right place; everything was turned over, thrown aside, broken into pieces, ruined. Panicked, I tried the door, but it was locked.

For a moment, I couldn't breathe. This door that had always been open to me was now closed. This house that had been so filled with warmth and goodness was now empty, lifeless, and mutilated. I gasped for air, choking. My cheeks were suddenly wet with tears.

That was when I finally understood that my friend was gone.

—

Buddha was the riderless horse at Mecca's funeral. She followed the horse-drawn carriage that carried the little white-and-gold coffin, Mecca's helmet attached to her saddle and her boots dangling backward in the stirrups.

The carriage drove slowly down the street to the church, the clip-clop of the horses' hooves echoing on the asphalt. Hundreds of people, some from the polo community who had seen Mecca play, some from the neighborhood, silently lined up on the sidewalks to watch the carriage pass. Dozens of Black Cowboys, saddled up and on their own horses, made a neighborhood honor guard, surrounding Buddha and Mecca on all sides.

—

The killer was never caught. There were rewards offered, posters stapled up everywhere, articles written for years afterward. Even for a community where death was no stranger, the murder of an entire family, and especially a beloved child like Mecca, was not something that could be ignored. Everyone knew that Mecca's stepfather had won $5,000 throwing dice just before they were shot—obviously the killer had been looking for that money—but that was as much as anyone could put together. Usually people talked on the streets and in the prisons, and we thought that eventually it was sure to come out. Someone would brag or drop a hint, maybe overhear something that would break it open. But no one ever so much as whispered a name. For all I know, the piece of shit who did it might still be walking around today, a free man.

—

For two years, Mecca and I had been secure in our own little world. We rode at the barn, getting better and better with each passing day. I watched her play on the team and tried as hard as I could to rise to her level. We slept in the hayloft and ran through the woods. When we weren't at the barn, we were wild in the streets. We stayed out as late as we liked, playing basketball, roller-blading, racing around from block to block. In the winter we'd come in earlier because it would get too cold, but in the summer there was never any curfew, except for the moment when we got so tired that we couldn't keep our eyes open anymore.

When I was with Mecca, the streets became our playground and our home.

At the end of the evening, more often than not, we'd both go back to Mecca's and curl up in her bed. We'd talk a little more, whispering in the dark so we wouldn't bother her mom and stepdad. And then, when we finally ran out of things to say, she'd sling an arm around me, lean her head against my shoulder, and we'd fall asleep that way, certain that we were safe and sacred, protected and adored.

CHAPTER NINE

Bee's coming home."

My mom was standing at the kitchen counter, cutting up an orange for Washika.

I thought I must have heard her wrong. "What did you say?"

"Bee. He coming home this weekend. For good."

For a moment, my heart leapt. *He knows. He knows how bad things are. He knows I need help.*

For a moment I thought he must be coming home for me.

"That Cissy woman don't want him no more. Says he's too much trouble."

I blinked. "What do you mean? He's been winning all over the place. Lezlie says he's probably going to get ranked as the number-one player in his age bracket."

"I'm not talking about polo." She shook her head. "He's acting up. They can't get him to mind. Says he's not listening. Missing school. The usual."

"So, they're forcing him to come home? He doesn't actually *want* to come back?"

She shrugged and set a plate of food down in front of my sister. "Doesn't really matter what he wants, now does it?"

—

Ever since Mecca died, I'd become afraid of the dark. The sun would go down, the streetlights would blink on, and a trickle of dread would ooze down my throat and settle in the pit of my stomach. I'd try to ignore it, to push it down. I'd watch TV until I was seeing double, I would desperately tease my mother and siblings to stay up just a little later. But night after night, after I dragged myself into the bedroom, I'd force myself to turn out the lights, and then silently begin to cry in fear. I had fallen into hell. I couldn't sleep, I couldn't talk, I couldn't move, and, more than anything, I felt like I couldn't breathe.

I was sure I was dying.

I'd lie there with my eyes squeezed shut, each breath more shallow than the last, overwhelmed with the absolute certainty that this was the end. No one could help me. Nothing could stop what was coming.

Of course, I had always been anxious. I was born vulnerable. I lived in an entire community of people who dealt with inherited trauma and constant loss. But this felt different. This was walking through my days under a cloud of low-level dread. This was lying there at night, filled with absolute panic, certain that if I let myself slip into sleep, I wouldn't ever wake up again.

It seemed like every week, there was a new death. Every time I turned a corner, there was a new memorial on the street.

Mike, a friend's older brother, was shot in a drive-by. Jigga, a middle-aged guy who always took a little time to clown with me when I passed him on the street corner, was killed in a bar fight. And with each new death, I was convinced that my own ending crept in just a little bit closer. People had been dying around me my whole life, and of course I didn't like it, but somehow I had always assumed I was immune. But now it was different. Because if Mike and Jigga could die—if Mecca could die—then I could die, too.

I imagined all the ways it could happen. On my way to the corner *papi* store, someone could aim, shoot, and miss— hitting me instead. It could happen walking to school; a speeding car could jump onto the sidewalk and mow me down. It could happen in my home; someone could break in and hold a gun to my head.

Or I could die in my bed, just lying there. My body could shut down, my heart could stop beating, and my lungs could refuse to work.

Years later I would finally have the vocabulary to explain what had been happening to me. I would be able to recognize PTSD and panic attacks and anxiety and depression. And I would look back on that freaked-out little kid, hyperventilating in the dark, and wish I could at least offer him the comfort of giving him the name for what he was going through.

But no one comforted me back then. No one even noticed what was happening. I finally got up the nerve to tell my mom, and she decided that I must have asthma. We went to the doctor for testing, and when all the tests came back negative, the doctor told my mom that there was nothing wrong with me. That it was all in my head. Fear and grief might be tangled into one giant, unbreakable knot, panic and sorrow choking me so hard that my breath couldn't get through, but it wasn't anything to worry about. Instead of offering tools or medication or even just recommending I might need some extra help, that doctor sent us on home, leaving me with the distinct feeling that he believed I was being overly dramatic and attention seeking.

The next time I had a panic attack, I just suffered through and kept it to myself.

But now, Bee was coming home. Bee was coming home and I was sure that he would bring everything I needed to knock away this fear. I was certain that having my big brother back in the house would allow me a measure of safety, that his presence would chase away my demons.

—

After two years in Texas, Bee didn't look like one of us anymore. The edges of his Wranglers were cut and frayed, he tucked in his T-shirt, he talked country. I'd never known anyone who had left and come back, and I was worried that the neighborhood would respond accordingly. I worried that it wouldn't matter that he was born and raised in The Bottom. He had gone away and returned different, and now maybe he was going to have to prove his place all over again.

I never asked him if he was happy to be home. Honestly, I was afraid to hear the answer. I had seen what he'd lost—the ponies, the beautiful farm, the elite polo life. Just a week in Fort Worth had made me look at things differently when I got back home; I couldn't imagine how it felt for Bee. But I understood enough to know that our shabby little barn in the park was a huge step backward for him.

When he walked back into our house that first day back, I watched him carefully, wondering if he realized what kind of danger he was in, if he felt some of the same fear that I couldn't shake. But Texas or not, he was still Bee, laughing, cocky, and brave. He still didn't seem to give a shit about what people thought.

I was relieved. I was certain that his fearlessness would make me brave, too. I was sure his confidence would be just what I needed to make it all better.

I waited for our family dinner to end, for Washika to be put down, for Bee to stop telling stories about Texas. For my mom to give him one more welcome-home hug before she went to bed. I thought we might watch some TV or talk a little more, but Bee said he was tired from the flight, so we all decided to turn in.

Gerb gave up his space next to me that night and slept on the floor so Bee could share my bed. We all got under our covers and turned out the light and I sighed with contentment, certain that everything would be okay again. We whispered for a bit, talking more about Texas, Bee telling us stories about the polo farm until Gerb and Kareema drifted off, and then, yawning, he reached over and patted me on the shoulder.

"Good night, bro," he said as he rolled over and closed his eyes.

He was sleeping so close I could feel the warmth coming off him. I could hear each singular breath he took, in and then out again. He was right there. It should have been enough. But as I closed my own eyes and tried to will myself to sleep, the fear came rolling in, thick and dense as it always was. Even with my brave older brother so close I could reach out and touch him, the panic and pain didn't dull. It was the same as always. I couldn't breathe. Bee or no Bee, it wrapped around me and took hold.

I got next to no sleep that night—unless you count blacking out from the fear and hyperventilation as rest—and I opened my eyes the next morning with a solid ball of anxiety filling my stomach. That weight stayed with me all day, keeping me constantly on the edge, ready for the worst to happen. The panic returned that night, and the next, and the next after that, too.

———

The only place the fear fell away was at the barn. As soon as I crossed into that warmth, that sweet, funky smell, as soon as I could lay hands on my pony, rest my brow against his neck, climb up on his back and ride so hard that the memories and panic couldn't keep up, I was free.

As usual, the horses and the barn were keeping me alive.

Lezlie was mad and worried that Bee had been sent back home, but I could tell that she was also a little excited to have him on the team. She came up with a new configuration that year. Bee was the captain, because of course he was the captain. A seventeen-year-old white boy named Andy who was a paying customer at the barn played number three, and I was given number one. Mecca's spot.

I couldn't decide if it was good or bad that I was playing for her. Mecca was a ghost on the field for me. I never rode when I didn't think of how she should have been there in my place, but I also never rode without playing as hard as I could. I had Bee to keep up with, but I had Mecca to live up to.

I couldn't be less than perfect if I was playing for both my brother and my lost friend. I was determined not to shame her memory.

—

And we didn't. With Bee carrying us, we traveled up and down the East Coast that whole polo season, and we played like no other Work to Ride team ever played before. We played and won at Cornell, Skidmore, Yale, the University of Virginia. We won the regional championship at Valley Forge in Wayne, Pennsylvania. Bee was the anchor and the star. Andy was good, and I was just thrilled to be along for the literal ride, but Bee was unstoppable.

Before this team, I had never won anything, and I had no idea that it could feel so amazing. When Bee whipped that ball through the goal posts and we took our first game, it felt like a promise. I was still a little kid, and we were playing high-school upperclassmen, and we were more than holding our own.

At the same time, Bee was back at home in the hood. All my worry about him not fitting in had proved baseless. Bee was no fool; he knew there was no tolerance for anyone being different on the streets. That Texas twang faded away in no time, the country boy disappeared, the clothes changed back to baggy jeans and oversized T-shirts, and Bee was a West Philly kid once more. That was when I learned that even if you leave the hood, The Bottom will always make some room and let you back in.

Bee was doing well at school and the barn. He knew he had fucked up in Texas and wanted to make things right with Lezlie, so he was working hard to keep to the rules. But sometimes, I'd see him standing on a street corner, laughing with his old friends, and I'd feel a different kind of worry take hold. I wished he was still wearing those Wranglers and maybe didn't fit in quite so well.

But on the field, watching him play, that worry faded away. I just saw a glorious future for us all. The streets didn't matter. He'd done what he promised—got his training, become the best—and now he was going to gallop straight on out of here and take us all with him just like he said he would.

Suddenly I remembered our family farm again, that cool, green, safe oasis. There would be nothing to fear there.

———

I was twelve years old, we were at the national championship at Cornell, and we were about to play the number-one-seeded team in the country. It was like a fever dream.

The opposing team was from Indio, California. The Eldorado Polo Club. The players were all seniors in high school, all children of professional polo players, and most of them were already carrying a four-goal handicap.

Bee was at a zero. Andy and I didn't even rank. Everyone was expecting us to be crushed. True, we had played well on the East Coast all season, but everyone knew that the best players were on the West Coast, and this particular team was the best of the best. No one thought we had a chance.

But Bee had spent two years in Texas riding every day on spectacular ponies, working with professional players, and getting the chance to hone the kind of talent that I truly believe only comes along maybe once in a generation. Riding against the best only made him better. From the moment the umpire bowled in the ball, Bee was on fire.

We matched that team goal for goal. And when I say "we" I mean, Bee. I'm sure that Andy and I made a couple of goals (probably set up like a birthday present from our captain) but really, we were basically there as window dressing. Bee was single-handedly dominating that game. He was everywhere, hooking and checking, goal after goal; offside, nearside, neckshot, he even made a pony goal. At one point, I caught myself just watching the faces of the opposing players as they watched him, their expressions shifting from disbelief to awe. Bee was full of fire and joy, and he was showing these guys how it was done.

Bee made another goal, and we pulled ahead by one. *We pulled ahead.* Andy and I looked at each other with matching grins of disbelief. I could hear Bee's shout of triumph all the way across the stadium, and then, just as we were all turning as one to switch goals, the lights went out, and the entire stadium went dark.

I froze. It was my worst fear come to find me in the one place I thought was impervious to its reach. All the charms against my panic were set up to protect me: I was on a pony, I was playing our beloved game, Lezlie was on the sidelines cheering us on, I was with my big brother, and we were winning, but it didn't matter. Darkness found me anyway.

It didn't last long. Emergency flashlights were pulled out and we led our ponies off the field and waited the fifteen or twenty minutes it took to restore the power and resume the game. The cold shock of panic I'd felt when the lights went out quickly dissipated and I shook off my unease. Still, once we were back on the field, we lost our momentum. Eldorado quickly retook the lead and beat us by three.

Losers or not, we went home proud that day. We had come in as underdogs, expecting to be wiped out and sent home early. Instead, we played the game that no one at the tournament could stop talking about. We had more than held our own against the best team in the country—in fact, we had very nearly won—and no one missed the fact that it had been the Killer Bee who had ruled the field.

After that tournament, Bee was ranked the best high-school player in the country. He was fourteen years old.

—

That following summer was one of the happiest times of my life. After the regionals and then the nationals, the polo world had lifted its head and finally taken notice of us. The season was over, but that didn't mean that folks weren't still playing games, and everyone wanted to see Bee do his thing. Lezlie could hardly handle the calls and requests that flooded in. Parents of kids we had played against, polo fans who had caught a chance game, people who had only just heard about us but wanted to see Bee for themselves—they all reached out and invited us to ride their ponies, play at their clubs, and stay in their homes. We got on the road and I don't remember returning home to Philly even once that summer.

You can't imagine what a Hamptons mansion looks like to a kid from The Bottom. Or how unequipped Bee and I were to be surrounded by this kind of money and luxury. On one hand, I was thrilled. These places overwhelmed me in the best possible way. When you're used to riding on fields full of cow wallows and divots, a perfectly groomed private playing field is a revelation. There's nothing to stop that ball from flying once you hit it on grass like that. When you learned to ride on ponies that threw you off as often as they carried you across the field, being seated on a hundred-thousand-dollar horse who had been trained from day one to do nothing but play felt like the equivalent of being handed a magic carpet. Everything felt so easy after learning it the hard way.

On the other hand, even though everyone was perfectly welcoming and warm, and we carried the shield of Bee's talent with us as we marched into these homes and rode out onto their fields, I was not stupid. I knew we were not prepared for this part of the world. I could see we were making mistakes. We traveled from estate to estate that summer, spending no more than three or four days at each place. People were kind and took an interest in us—they recognized our talent—but I couldn't help but feel that we were the entertainment. We knew that people were curious about where we came from, that our background was part of the attraction, but we didn't want to talk about any of the real stuff we were going through back home. There wasn't much impulse to be honest about where we lived when we were standing in the middle of some kid's bedroom that was bigger than the whole first floor of our house. And besides, we were in and out of most of these places. There wasn't ever enough time to get comfortable.

I didn't like feeling like the hired clown, I didn't like making mistakes, so I decided that the best thing we could do was learn. As was my habit, I hung back and watched things carefully and it quickly became clear to me that we didn't know the first thing about how to behave and that I needed to hurry up and figure out what we needed to change.

Meals were the worst. Lezlie glared at us from across the table as we blithely reached across our host's plate to serve ourselves, or picked up the wrong fork, or chewed with our mouths open. Learning proper table manners was obviously something we needed to do. Pools were not much better. We'd never had the chance to learn to swim, so Bee and I would plant ourselves in the shallow end, splashing and yelling and making a ruckus, hoping to distract from the fact that we didn't dare go in above our belly buttons. I secretly watched the other kids swim, thinking maybe I could figure out how it was done.

Lezlie had been telling us to take more pride in our appearance for years, but it was only now that everyone around us was clothed in perfect whites and thousand-dollar boots, their ponies clipped and braided and groomed until they shined, their tack cleaned and polished by professional grooms, that we finally started feeling like maybe she'd been right all along. We wanted to look better, act better, fit in.

It made us hungry.

So we watched. Imitated. Tucked in our shirts and took a little more time polishing our boots. Listened to Lezlie and kept our mouths shut and minded our p's and q's as best we could so we wouldn't embarrass her. Sometimes we forgot. Sometimes we got wild or snatched up things that weren't ours and broke them without thinking. Sometimes we didn't say thank you and Lezlie would have to throw an elbow as we walked out the door so that we'd remember. But we tried, and learned, and maybe we weren't always the best house-guests, but we always redeemed ourselves on the field. Bee was fierce, dangerous poetry on horseback, and that's all they really seemed to want from us anyway.

By the end of the summer, when we had to return to The Bottom and our barn, we had changed. We had a new world to measure our old one against, and it was suddenly hard not to see just how small our old world really was.

CHAPTER TEN

Years after the fact, when I finally got up the nerve to ask Bee why he quit polo, he had to remind me that he was still a child when he walked away, and that children generally can't be counted on to make the best decisions for themselves.

"It's not like it happened all at once," he said. "I didn't wake up one morning and think, 'Okay, that's it! I'm done!' It happened bit by bit. I wanted a nice phone, and I knew that if I hustled a little, I could buy one. I wanted to skip school and not have to answer to a pissed-off Lezlie when she found out. Some days I just didn't want to wake up early and go out in the cold and shovel shit, so I'd stay in bed instead. I was a kid. I was making my decisions minute to minute. I didn't understand that every time I broke a rule or showed up late or left early, I was fucking up my entire future. I just wanted what I wanted. I thought I'd always have my talent when I needed it, I'd always have access to the ponies when I wanted them. I was sure I'd always have another chance to play again when I was ready. I knew that Lezlie was tough and I was testing her patience hard, but I never believed that she'd actually tell me to go and never come back.

"Lezlie always talked about how polo was going to get us out of the hood, but I didn't see the path. Polo isn't football or basketball. Polo was never going to make me rich. I mean, you actually need to be rich to ride in the first place. It was a little bit of a joke. I was the best in the nation, but so what? What did that get me? Were there endorsements? Was anyone recruiting me for anything? Every time we'd play a game or walk into a club, all I could see was that everyone around us had so fucking much, and we had nothing.

"I didn't want to be the kid with nothing anymore."

———

What do you do when someone goes from being your idol to being held up as a cautionary tale?

He made his choice. That was the party line. I must have heard it said, and said it myself, a hundred times after Bee left the barn. I didn't think anything could ever hurt as much as losing Mecca, but losing Bee came pretty fucking close. At least when Mecca died, I was allowed to be sad. I was allowed to miss her. With Bee, I was just supposed to shake my head at the waste of talent and potential, and do everything I could to *not* be him. Which wasn't easy, since I had spent pretty much all of my life wishing I could be exactly like my big brother.

———

It felt like a tragedy, but it didn't happen in a particularly dramatic way. It happened slowly. Over the course of a year.

First it was all three of us—me, Bee, and Kareema, playing hooky from school together. We'd go out the door with our mom in the morning and then peel off when she turned the corner for work, and double back to the house. That quickly became a bad habit. There was one month that winter when we skipped twenty-four days, total. Eventually Lezlie got wind of this and brought down the hammer. She took away the horses and the games. We couldn't play, we couldn't ride, we were banned from anything fun. For Kareema and me, those kinds of consequences were still enough to set us back on track, but for Bee, it just made him stubborn and resentful. Just like David, Bee didn't want to be told what to do or be punished when he did wrong.

Then he started skipping at the barn. He'd miss practice, he'd miss games, and suddenly we were losers again. Lezlie would have to grab whoever was hanging around the barn to substitute for him, and that never ended well. It was chaos on the field. And even when Bee did appear, he was always already in trouble for missing school or not showing up on previous barn days, so Lezlie wouldn't let him play then, either.

After that, it was a quick slide into the streets. Bee started hanging out with friends who weren't from the barn, he was hustling and making some money, he came back home less and less, he was pulled in by the cops a couple of times, and one day—a day I can't even remember, it was so ordinary—he walked out of the barn for the last time and never came back again.

——

There is no doubt that Bee broke Lezlie's heart. She loved him like she loved all of us—probably even more—and it must have been horrible to see a kid with such talent and promise slip back into the streets. But Lezlie never thought of herself as a savior. She knew that for every kid like Bee—a kid so talented she could pull strings to get him sent to live on a fancy polo farm, a kid who got invited into mansions and exclusive clubs—there were hundreds more who just needed the barn for someplace warm and safe to go after school and on the weekends. She knew that Work to Ride wasn't going to get everyone—or even most of us—out of the hood, but she hoped that maybe it would at least give some kids the incentive to stay in school a little longer than they would have otherwise, or maybe try a little harder to keep their grades up while they were there. Lezlie had studied psychology and had been around horses her whole life. She inherently understood that horses could ease trauma, and that pretty much every kid from our neighborhood had been traumatized. She wanted to help as many of us as possible in whatever way she could, but she knew she could only do so much. So while I'm sure that Lezlie grieved for Bee, she just didn't have the luxury of hurting too long over any one child. There were always dozens more waiting for her attention. Maybe not with Bee's talent, but certainly with as much need as he ever had. Lezlie's way of coping with loss was to double down on the kids she had left in her care.

I wanted to talk to Bee, to ask him why he had done it, to beg him to come back and follow the barn rules, but it wasn't like when he left for Texas. We were older now, for one thing, and Bee was just doing what almost all the boys in our neighborhood grew up to do. He was learning a new game. He was following a different set of rules. He was taking the place on the street that had always been there waiting for him.

When Bee left for Texas, it was sad, but it didn't feel like a betrayal. I'd understood that he was leaving for all of us, in a way. When Bee left the barn, that was a much harder blow. He wasn't just rejecting Lezlie and Work to Ride, he was giving up on our future. He was leaving the family team.

After Bee left, my panic attacks ramped up worse than ever. I began spending my nights not only imagining how I would die, but also how Bee would go, too. If Bee wasn't home, and he wasn't at the barn, that meant that I needed to worry about him. That meant that he wasn't safe.

The only time I could push my feelings away was when I was playing. So I did what Lezlie wanted. I followed the barn rules so I could play as much and as hard as I possibly could. It paid off in some ways; I was learning and getting stronger as a player, but I was sinking in almost every other way. I got better at polo as I got worse at surviving, and I think Lezlie saw that.

———

"His name is Cholo," said Lezlie.

The sleek bay thoroughbred flicked his tail as he looked at me. He was brand-new to the barn, but didn't have the nervous energy a new pony usually brought with him. This horse already seemed content to be there.

I took a step toward the gelding and scratched him on the neck. He leaned toward me when I touched him, and shoved his nose under my hand when I stopped, asking for more. "Where'd he come from?" I asked.

"Off the track," said Lezlie. "He's still a baby, four years old. The only thing he knows how to do is turn left and run without stopping."

I raised my eyebrows. "And you think he'll make a good polo pony?"

Lezlie shrugged. "I think he will if you train him to be one."

I stopped scratching him. "Me?"

"You train him, and when I sell him, we'll put any profit we make into your college fund."

I laughed. "Like I have a college fund."

"Well, this can be the beginning of it, then."

I looked at the horse again, admiring the perfect white star on his forehead. "You really think I can train a horse?"

Lezlie nodded. "It's mostly about patience. You have plenty of that."

Cholo stretched his neck and delicately nibbled on my collar; I gently pushed him away to save my shirt, and then reached over and rubbed the star. His eyes immediately went half-mast with pleasure.

"Look at that," said Lezlie. "He likes you already."

"Okay," I said, trying to sound as if it was no big deal. "Okay, I guess I can try."

———

There is nothing like the feeling you get when a horse chooses you.

Horses are prey animals. They spend their lives basically waiting to be run down and eaten, so it's not really in their nature to trust. Some horses never warm up to people at all; they might tolerate someone riding them and show up when you rattle the feed bucket, but they're still going to give you the side-eye every time you approach. Some horses act like they're just waiting for you to show your true colors and take out your knife and fork to dig in.

Cholo, on the other hand, was basically a Labrador re-
triever in a horse's body. He loved and trusted me from the
moment I met him. Even that first day when I took him out
to the ring, I could drop the lead and walk ahead and he'd
follow along like a baby duck after his mama. Compared to
Buck, who still liked to throw me off if I wasn't paying close
enough attention, Cholo made me feel he was in it with me
from the start.

He needed a lot of training, though. Lezlie hadn't been
joking when she said that all a racehorse knows how to do is
turn left and run. The first thing I had to teach him was how
to stop. I took him up into a canter, just to see what would
happen, and I thought we'd ride the fence forever. We just
kept circling and circling, with me sawing on the reins, until
he finally wore himself out and slowed to a halt.

When I started training Cholo, I thought a lot about Angel, my first pony. Angel had taught me how to ride. She was
patient and forgiving and willing to put up with my lack of
experience. She knew what I was trying to ask from her even
when I didn't exactly know how to make it clear. She made
me feel safe and understood. I wanted to teach Cholo like
Angel had taught me.

Training a horse is all about repetition. You have to know
how to ride, and how to use your body to tell the pony what
you want, and then you just repeat yourself until it becomes
muscle memory for you both. Some people think you need to
"break" a horse, that a horse needs to be a little afraid of its
rider in order to get him to mind, but that's never been my
experience. My experience is that a horse will respect you
if you ride them properly. You can't let them be in charge,
but if you are clear, and you are firm but gentle, and you are

willing to keep trying to communicate until the horse understands, you will end up with an animal who can happily be taught just about anything.

Cholo was a perfect example of this. He was so smart, so willing to learn, and all he really wanted was to please me. He was the exactly the right size, build, and temperament for polo, and I could not wait to get him out on a field. Our team, such as it was, had been knocked out of the tournament early that year—without Bee we hadn't stood a chance—so there were no weekend games to ride in, and certainly no invitations to the Hamptons to look forward to. The barn, and my life, had gone quiet without Mecca or my brother in it. Training Cholo made a little noise. It kept me distracted. That horse was a small spot of warmth in an otherwise frozen landscape. Lezlie giving him to me made it seem like my future wasn't quite so lost.

—

There were times when I wondered if I was doomed to follow David and Bee into the streets. I didn't want to. The family had always joked about me being too scared for the life, and they weren't wrong. But when I thought about Bee, who'd had so much more talent, potential, and opportunity than me and still couldn't resist the pull, I didn't really see how I was supposed to be the one who finally stood firm.

My father had been sitting in an empty lot, drinking his days away, for as long as I could remember. I passed him nearly every day, and he never looked up from his bottle, never bothered to say a word to me. I imagine he must have wanted more than that at some point. I imagine that he must have had dreams or plans. But when you live where we lived, it was just easier to give in. We were given a path, a road, a map to follow; but it didn't lead us out of The Bottom, it led us to the street corner or to the empty lot or to prison or an early grave. We were surrounded by death and violence, pumped full of despair until we turned numb, taught we were expendable. It was no wonder that David was in prison, that Mecca was killed, that Bee got swallowed back into the streets. The flames that burned the brightest in my world were being extinguished around me, one by one.

—

"Lez! Lezlie! Lez! Watch this!"

Cholo and I were racing across the soccer field. I was leaning out of my saddle, sending the ball ahead of us with sharp, controlled taps from my mallet. We swerved left and then right, weaving our way around our imaginary opponents. Cholo felt like a dream, as good as any of the horses I had ridden in the Hamptons or upstate New York. He sensed what I wanted before I could make a move to tell him, he could turn—in any direction now—in an instant, he ran with all his heart. He and I were perfectly in sync.

We made one last swerve and I sent the ball flying between the goal posts, winning the Argentine Open in my mind.

"That was amazing!" Lezlie cheered as I trotted Cholo to the sideline where she was standing and brought him to a halt. "I can't believe how much progress you've made!"

I leaned over and patted his neck. "It's all him."

Lezlie grinned at me. "He's a natural, eh? He's going to be worth a lot."

I frowned, suddenly uneasy with the way she was describing him.

"At this rate, he'll be ready to sell much sooner than we thought. You've already made such a difference with him. I'm so proud of you!"

—

Sometimes I liked to forget about the fact that Cholo was not really my horse. Sometimes I liked to imagine that he would be the first of my string of ponies. That someday I would ride him as I made the winning goal at nationals. That much later, he would retire to the greenest, lushest pasture on my farm, where maybe he'd teach my own kids to ride like Angel had taught me. I would visit him every day and bring him an apple and scratch his nose where it had gone gray.

Sometimes I just liked to imagine that someone— anyone—I loved could stay.

CHAPTER ELEVEN

Considering I grew up in a place that often felt like a war zone, I suppose it was no surprise that someone thought I'd make a good soldier.

The campus of Valley Forge Military Academy was lush, green, and manicured. The stately, elegant buildings were either red brick or painted a crisp, bright white. There were one hundred acres of rolling hills and wide paths, and it had the biggest indoor riding ring on the East Coast. It was the arena where Bee, Andy, and I had beaten the pants off the Valley Forge polo team on more than one occasion.

Sometimes when we won a game, the opposing team would be nasty about it. I heard bitter comments about how we'd just been lucky, or that the umps had favored us because they felt sorry for us. I'd experienced rolled eyes and reluctant handshakes after the game was over. But the Valley Forge team was never like that. The guys on that team, boys who were much richer and older than us, just seemed

impressed whenever we won. They smiled at us and compli-
mented us on a good game, they remarked on particularly
slick moves Bee had made. After we put away the ponies,
they offered to show us around the campus and hang out for
a while. They were warm and friendly and fun. They told us
hilarious stories about trying to escape from campus and live
a normal non-military-school life. Even if they weren't the
greatest on horseback, I liked those cadets.

And I guess they must have liked me, too, because just before my eighth-grade year, Lezlie got a call at the barn. It
seemed that those same boys we had beaten had gone to their
parents and insisted that I should be going to their school and
playing on their polo team. And their parents must have listened, because suddenly, I was being offered a full ride to the
academy.

"You're going," said Lezlie. "This is your chance. What
have I always told you to do when you got your chance?"

"You told me to get out," I said.

"And?"

"Stay out," I finished.

There was no arguing. The two things that Lezlie stressed
above all else were the importance of a good education and
that if any of us ever got the chance, we would get the hell
out of The Bottom and never look back.

My mom agreed. My mom always agreed with Lezlie,
sometimes to the point where people in the neighborhood
would call her out for putting such trust in a white lady from
outside the hood. "How come you let that woman tell you
what to do with your kids?" they'd ask my mom. But my
mom would just shrug and change the subject. She told me
that she always knew that Lezlie was our best chance to make

it out. She felt lucky to have another adult in our lives who cared about us as much as Lezlie did. So if Lezlie said I was going to military school, that's where I was going.

Honestly, I didn't mind. Aside from Cholo, I couldn't see much to keep me in Philly anymore. David, Bee, and Mecca were all gone, our current team sucked, I was barely sleeping at night, I still couldn't even walk down to the corner in my neighborhood without falling to pieces, and the only reason I even bothered going to school was so Lezlie would let me ride.

I liked the boys I knew at VF. I liked the way the campus looked. It was clean and quiet. It felt safe and orderly. I'd seen some of the dorm rooms and they were bigger than the bedroom I was still sharing with three of my siblings back home. And more than anything, I coveted those fancy ponies and that indoor riding arena. It was the same thing that Bee had been offered when he went to Texas—the chance to ride every day, rain, snow, or shine. Why would I ever put up a fight?

So I agreed to go, but one thing gave me pause: Kareema and Gerb and Washika. Nobody was offering them any scholarships. They would be left behind, and I remembered all too well how that felt.

"You really going?" asked Gerb. His eyes were worried.

I nodded. It was early on a Saturday morning, and we were all walking to the barn together.

"Won't you miss home?" asked Kareema.

I shrugged. "I won't be that far away. Lezlie says that after the first six weeks I can come back to visit on the weekends if I want."

Kareema wrinkled her nose. "What happens during that first six weeks?"

I shook my head. "All I know is that you're not allowed to make any phone calls or see anyone from home."

"And that doesn't seem weird to you?" asked Gerb.

"I'm sure it's fine," I said. "Listen, after I graduate, I'll be in the position to help you guys, too."

Kareema rolled her eyes. "Yeah, that's what Bee said when he went to Texas."

"I'm not Bee," I said automatically.

Gerb laughed. "No fucking kidding."

I gave him a little shove, annoyed. "You guys will be okay without me. Just stick to the barn. Don't break the rules."

Kareema snorted. "Okay, Lezlie. Whatever you say."

"I'll miss you, Reem," said Gerb. He was so quiet, I almost didn't hear him say it.

For a moment I almost changed my mind. How could I leave them behind? Who was going to watch out for them? Who was going to make sure that they didn't run wild and screw it all up for themselves?

Then I imagined what would happen if I told Lezlie that I couldn't go.

I slung an arm around Gerb's shoulder and met my sister's eyes. "Just keep riding," I said. "Everything will be okay if you guys keep riding."

Kareema shook her head but smiled.

Gerb nodded. "I know. I will."

—

Lezlie and Mom drove me up to the school. It was a warm, beautiful August day. Sunny and clear. As we pulled in and parked, we might as well have been going to Disneyland, I was so excited. The campus was clean and orderly; not a blade of grass looked out of place. I craned my neck to look down the hill at the stable and paddocks, anxious to see the horses. Around me, new cadets from all over the world were pouring out of their cars, slamming their doors, and blinking in the bright sunlight. I had heard talk that there were actual princes and royalty who would be attending with me.

The first day at the school started out fairly easy. We were divided into units and introduced to our squad leader, a blond, stocky upperclassman named Tyler Banks. I was surprised to realize that there were very few actual adults around. All my direct supervisors seemed to be teenagers. Granted, they were highly disciplined, very stern, and regimented teenagers, but they were still just kids who were allowed to tell me what to do.

The returning cadets escorted us to our barracks where we were stripped of our civilian clothes and told to change into our "PT" (physical training) uniform: a gray T-shirt and shorts, white socks, black sneakers. After that, we were taken to the barber, where I stood in line until it was my turn to get my head shaved.

Both of my older brothers had been in and out of jail at this point. They had come back from juvie and prison with stories that made me sick to my stomach, always starting with having everything they owned taken from them, being put into prison uniforms, and then being made to shave their heads. Every time they told those stories, I had sworn to myself that it would never be me. That I would be the one in our family who didn't get locked away. So when it was my turn to sit in the barber's chair and have my head shaved, shit suddenly started to get real in a way I hadn't been expecting.

It's not a prison, I told myself as I rubbed my now completely bald head. *It's just a school.*

After our haircuts, we were assembled in front of our parents again to learn a few drills. The drills were hard for me to master at first. I struggled trying to get all the moves right and on time, but the drill leaders were patient. They smiled as they helped us learn. I should have been relieved as they slowly moved us from clumsy formation to clumsy formation, but there was something in their expressions that I didn't trust. Their smiles didn't reach their eyes. I knew the look of trouble coming; I had seen it all my life. And these big white boys with their fancy uniforms and fake grins were making me nervous.

After the drills were finally done, we were marched to the parade field where the parents were seated and we plebes stood in formation and listened to a welcoming speech from the president of the school. I remember nothing about that speech except that I was hot standing in the sun and I didn't like the way my newly shorn head made me feel exposed and foolish.

After the speech, we were sworn in as cadets. I honestly don't remember much about that, either, except that I knew I was getting closer and closer to the moment when I would have to say goodbye to my mom and Lezlie, and take on whatever was coming next.

—

"You do good here, okay? You show these boys what you're made of," said my mother as she pulled me into a tight hug. "I'm so proud of you, Reem. I love you so much."

"Love you, too," I mumbled into her shoulder.

"You write me and I'll write you back," said Lezlie as she took her turn hugging me. "Get down to those stables and ride. Call me as soon as you can."

I gave them both a wavering grin, trying not to think too hard about the fact that I would be completely cut off from them and everyone I knew for a whole six weeks.

It's just a school, not a prison, I reminded myself again as I watched them turn and wave at me one last time before they walked back down to the car and drove away.

—

"Let's go, you dirty fucking plebes!" screamed our squad leader as soon as the last parent had disappeared. "Mess hall! On the double! GO! GO! GO!"

The thing that I hadn't quite realized before this moment was that the students literally ran the school. The ranked upperclassmen were not only in charge of our training, but they were also in charge of our punishment and the judicial system, such as it was, that doled it out. Aside from academic classes, there were basically no adults around to keep things under control. We were at the absolute mercy of the upperclassmen, and it became very clear, very quickly, that they didn't have any mercy at all.

Suddenly I wanted nothing so much as I wanted to race back down the hill, find my mom and Lezlie, and demand that I be allowed to go back home.

—

At dinner, the extent of the rules that were now going to shape our lives started to become clear. I could hardly believe it, but they were going to dictate exactly how we ate.

"You need to sit exactly six inches forward in your seat," barked the squad leader. "Square off your tray! Put your forks down while you chew, keeping your hands to your sides until you swallow each bite! If someone approaches the table, you will lock it up! This means stop whatever you're doing, put down your utensils, put your arms to your sides, and stare straight ahead. No eye contact!"

He put his big red face directly into the face of the boy across from me, a small kid with blotchy skin who looked like he was on the verge of tears.

"I SAID NO EYE CONTACT!" our squad leader screamed into this kid's face. Little droplets of spit landed on his cheeks.

The squad leader stood back up. "If someone addresses you, you will either say 'No, sir!' Or 'Yes, sir!' If I hear you speaking in any other way, you will be sorry you spoke at all! Do you understand?"

"Yes, sir!" we mumbled.

"I said, do you fucking weak-ass plebes UNDERSTAND?"

"YES, SIR!" we responded in kind.

By the time we were done with training, dinnertime was over and I had barely eaten a bite.

"Back to your dorms, plebes!" yelled our squad leader, and we were all up and running just like that.

—

"You have two minutes to change and then two minutes to shower!" Banks shouted at us.

I tried not to look at my roommate, a heavyset guy with dark hair who I hadn't even had any time to introduce myself to yet, as I slipped out of my PT and into my robe and shower shoes. At the last second, it occurred to me that I might have to take a public shower with all the other boys, so I kept my underwear on just in case.

"LET'S GO! LET'S GO!" came our squad leader's voice from out in the hall.

My roommate and I grabbed our shower caddies and stumbled out into the hall.

"You should be standing at attention, YOU FUCKING MORONS!" shouted Banks as he and a bunch of the other upperclassmen marched up and down the hall and shoved people into proper formation.

I quickly threw my shoulders back and put my arms down at my sides, trying to figure out just where my middle finger should be resting based on the fact that I was wearing a bath-robe.

"Chin up! Chest out! Shoulders back! Stomach in, you fucknuts!"

The teens cruised up and down the hallway, pinching and pulling us plebes into shape. Suddenly one of the them stopped in front of a short, red-haired kid. "Where are your shower shoes, Plebe?"

The redhead looked terrified. "Um. I couldn't—I don't think I have any . . . sir."

Banks's head spun around, and he strode down the hall, shoving the other upperclassman out of the way. "Oh no," he said to the redheaded kid. "You couldn't find your flip-flops?" For a moment his voice sounded almost kind, but no one could miss the sadistic gleam in his eyes.

"N-no, sir," said the kid. "I think my mama forgot to pack them maybe, sir?"

Every kid in that hallway flinched when he said it. We all knew just what a huge mistake he had made. The kid himself closed his eyes in horror as soon as the words came out of his mouth.

Banks stared at the kid with a huge, mean-as-fuck grin plastered on his face. "Your mama? YOUR MAMA FORGOT YOUR SHOES? Are you fucking kidding me with this shit, Plebe?"

"N-no, sir. I mean—"

Banks stuck his index finger into the kid's chest. The kid squinted in pain. "You listen to me, Plebe. First thing in the morning, you are going to run barefoot for me until I say stop. And I don't care if you puke. And I don't care if those feet bleed. And I don't care if you fall down and fucking die. You will go until I fucking say stop. And If I ever, EVER hear you mention your 'mama' again, I will make it my pet project to get you kicked out of this school and home to your fucking 'mama' within the week. DO YOU UNDERSTAND, PLEBE?"

The kid looked like he was going to throw up right then and there, but he managed to squeak out, "Yes, sir."

"ALL RIGHT, THEN!" screamed Banks. "Get to the goddamned showers!"

And we ran.

———

The shower was miserable. It was, as I feared, completely public, and I felt stupid keeping my underwear on, but I couldn't bring myself to be naked in a room full of strangers. We had two minutes. The squad leader stood outside the shower stalls and counted down as I tried desperately to rinse the soap out of my eyes and then raced back into my bathrobe, soaking wet and dripping on the floor, before he got to zero.

That night we learned how to stand (head down) out in the hallway during taps, which was played over the intercom at exactly ten o'clock. As soon as taps was finished, we were told to get into our beds and all the lights went out and we were plunged into darkness.

My roommate was probably around three hundred pounds. He had offered me the upper bunk with a wave of his hand. I had gathered that his name was Luca and he was from Colombia, and it was obvious that he was at the school completely against his will. He started to sob the moment he hit the sheets, and I lay there listening to him for the next forty-five minutes straight.

One thing the school was very careful about was keeping everyone hydrated. They shoved bottles of water at us all day long, and the squad leaders would stand there and make sure you drank them. I must have gulped down ten bottles that day. As I lay there in the dark, I should have been crying, too. I should have felt as tired and hungry and scared and homesick as my roommate obviously was. But instead, all I could concentrate on was the fact that I really, really had to take a piss.

"Luca?" I whispered. He had finally stopped sobbing. "Do you know if we're allowed to go to the bathroom after reveille?"

Silence.

I closed my eyes, thinking maybe I could just stop thinking about it and go to sleep.

No such luck.

"Luca?"

I was pretty sure I was going to burst. I didn't want to wet my bed, but the thought of running into our squad leader when I wasn't supposed to be out of my room was too terrifying to contemplate.

Finally, I remembered that there was an empty water bottle on my desk. I crept down the ladder to my bunk, felt my way across the room, groped for the bottle, and felt sweet, immense relief as I pissed into it, hoping that Luca was a deep enough sleeper not to wake up and catch me in the act. When I was done, I screwed the cap back on and stuck the bottle under my desk, reminding myself that I must find a way to get it out of the room before someone found it tomorrow. Then I made my way back across the room and up the ladder, slipped back into the sheets, and, just for the tiniest moment, enjoyed the fact that I had a whole bed to myself. Then, before I could worry or forget to breathe or start to cry, I was asleep.

—

"WAKE UP! WAKE UP! WAKE UP! GET THE FUCK OUT OF BED!"

It was still dark and someone was kicking at our door so hard that I was sure it would burst open any moment. I looked at the illuminated alarm clock by my bunk. It was 4:30 in the morning.

"Rise and shine, you little shitheads! You have ten seconds to get out here and stand at attention! Anyone who takes longer than ten seconds will be cleaning the floor with a toothbrush and their tongue!"

I jumped out of bed, terrified, rushing past my roommate, stumbling out into the pitch-black hallway.

Suddenly the lights came on all at once and it was a repeat

of the night before, the upperclassmen prowling the hall as we all blinked under the buzzing fluorescent lights, doing our best not to look ridiculous in our nightclothes and military posture. I looked at the line of plebes out of the corners of my eyes. Apparently some of them slept in their underwear, and at least one of them slept in nothing at all.

"This is disgusting!" yelled our squad leader. "I am fucking embarrassed for you plebes! You have two minutes to get dressed. Move it! NOW!"

—

If you force a bunch of kids to run long enough and hard enough, and you don't let them rest and you don't let them slow down, eventually one of them will puke. And after the first one pukes, you can count on the next one puking, and then another, and another, until you're a bunch of spewing dominos playing a never-ending game of I-see-what-you-ate-for-dinner-last-night.

Years of working in the barn had left me in better shape than most of the other plebes, but by the time the sun came up, we had been running for hours, and even I felt like I was dying. Every thirty minutes or so, they would stop us and force us drop and do pushups until we puked all over again or collapsed, and then they'd make us haul ourselves back up and run some more.

Finally, at the point where I was pretty sure I was going to pass out or die, our squad leader stopped us, lined us up, and yelled, "ALL RIGHT YOU FUCKING MAGGOTS! TIME FOR YOUR FIRST TRAINING! LET'S GO! LET'S GO!"

We learned how to march that day: Step off straight ahead with your left foot, thirty inches forward. Heel on ground.

Swing your right arm forward at the same time, nine inches forward and six inches back. Repeat with right foot and left arm. I had no idea that marching was so precise.

We were finally allowed to eat breakfast. In the mess, we all sat down, exhausted, but then straightened up when we realized that we were being watched like hawks to make sure we followed all the rules perfectly. If anyone messed up, they'd have their tray taken away and be told to do pushups right there on the floor. I managed to avoid punishment that morning, but this was also when I realized that the food at VF was complete garbage. I had only ever been told what prison food was like, but I was fairly certain it couldn't be worse than the slop I was forcing down.

We were given our cap shield books—fourteen slim pamphlets that we were told we must memorize and prove our mastery of within the next six weeks. They contained everything from the military ranking system to the school's alma mater. As soon as you memorized one pamphlet you could request that your squad leader listen to you recite, and if you passed the test and he signed off, you were given a privilege.

We were starting out with nothing. No communication with the outside world. No free time. No food outside what we ate in the mess. Your family might send you a package, but the upperclassmen would open it right in front of you and consume or destroy whatever they found as you watched. Every minute, every second, of our lives was dictated and controlled. We were screamed at constantly. There were no academic classes for the first two weeks. We saw no adults, just upperclassmen who obviously took great joy in making us as scared and miserable as possible. We were forced to march and run drills nonstop, and if anyone messed up, the rest of us would pay for that fuckup while the guilty kid watched; it was called getting "smoked," which meant they'd exercise us until we either puked or collapsed.

The upperclassmen were beyond cruel to us. It was *Lord of the Flies* on steroids. They bullied us and cursed us out and pushed us past endurance and laughed when we got hurt and didn't show us one moment of softness or understanding. I loathed them.

After reveille that second night, my roommate Luca started crying, and this time, I was right there with him. We both sobbed through the night as I thought about what a huge mistake I had made agreeing to come to this shithole of a school, as I imagined slipping out and running away, as I thought, *Maybe this really is a prison.*

I was miserable and homesick and exhausted and freaked out, but, as I finally drifted off to sleep, I realized something: maybe I was crying, maybe I was angry and upset and deeply regretful of the choices I had made, maybe I was physically exhausted—but I wasn't really scared. Despite the darkness, there was no panic attack. This school sucked. I hated it. I hated every single thing about it. But a bunch of rich, white bullies were nothing compared to where I had come from and what I knew to be possible. All this abuse and screaming and yelling, all these "privileges" taken away from us, it just felt performative and clownish. It was a weird facsimile of true deprivation. I knew what the worst was—I had lived among the worst possible things every single day of my life—and this was like playing a video game or watching a movie of those things. I wasn't happy, but I was fairly certain that no one was going to kill me at this school, either. I desperately wanted to go home, but not because I thought I couldn't survive where I was.

Even the dark here was different. Every night all the lights would go off at once, and the darkness was darker than at home. It was pitch black. But this darkness didn't feel like it was hiding anything. It wasn't menacing or suffocating like it had been back in my room. In fact, it was a relief. When it was dark, I could finally let go and cry and nobody would see or scream at me for doing it. When it was dark, I could rest for the first time all day. It granted me the only privacy I was allowed. It felt protective and restorative. It felt like a reprieve.

Luca went home by the end of the week. He collapsed while we were running up Suicide Hill (so named for obvious reasons) and I never saw him again. By the time I got back to our barracks that night, his desk and bureau were empty and he was gone. We hadn't really gotten to know each other—his English wasn't great and my Spanish was nonexistent—but I did feel a pang of regret to see him go. He and I had quietly wept together every night for the first week of school, and that was not nothing when it came to shared experiences.

———

When I completed my third cap shield test in our second week, I was finally allowed to go to a polo practice. I practically ran to the stables. I'd been dying to get to the horses from the moment I first arrived, and the dusty, hay-sweet scent of the barn smelled like pure freedom.

My two teammates were Dylan Jones and Richard Harris.

They were rich, white seniors from Connecticut and Alabama. Their parents had donated a shit ton of money to the school, and they were the reason I was there. I had beat them on the field at least twice, and they had decided that they wanted me on their team.

The thing was, though, they were also highly ranked upperclassmen, and they had spent the previous two weeks getting in my face and screaming at me every time we crossed paths. I understood this to some degree; upperclassmen did not fraternize with plebes, and even though they knew I'd be their teammate, they couldn't show any favoritism. But it wasn't exactly the greatest way to kick off a season or build team spirit.

So it was with a mix of resentment and glee that I got into the saddle and rode into the ring with them. As soon as I was on a pony, the tables turned. The arena felt like it was *mine*. I was not captain of this team, but I had been brought in as a ringer. I was thirteen years old and everybody knew that I could whip—and had whipped—both their asses on horseback.

Now you're going to fucking listen to me, I thought as we begin to ride. They'd been treating me like shit for days, and now I could finally take it to them. I didn't say a word. I let my riding speak for me. For an hour, we rode and played hard, and I dominated them. I hooked their mallets and forced them into rideoffs and stole the ball and made goal after goal right under their noses. For an hour, I had pride and felt in control and saw myself as a human being again. Then I put away my pony and rejoined my unit and went back to being the shit on everyone's shoe.

The next time Jones and Harris saw me, though, they still screamed and yelled and cussed me out, but there was something in their expressions that was different. There was something that made it clear that all this was temporary and would be over soon enough.

——

I had been writing to Lezlie for weeks. It was the only communication I was allowed and all my letters were the same: *I hate it here. I want to come home. This place sucks. Why did you make me come?*

In my fifth week, I received my cap shield and was finally allowed to make a phone call. I hesitated for a moment and then dialed the barn.

"Lez?"

"Kareem!" she said. Her voice was the warmest thing I'd heard for five weeks.

All of a sudden I was swamped with homesickness. My voice started to shake. "Lez, I hate this place. I want to come home," I pleaded.

"Didn't you just make it through the worst part? You've only got one more week before you graduate from being a plebe."

I swallowed. I knew this. In fact, before I had called her, I was feeling pretty great. Finally getting my cap shield had been a huge accomplishment and relief. But hearing her voice brought all my feelings of regret and loneliness swimming to the surface. I missed the barn and our horses. I missed Gerb and Washika and Kareema. I missed Lezlie and my mom. I wanted my freedom.

"I can't do this anymore," I said. "This place sucks. I don't belong here."

"Kareem," she returned. "What have I told you a million times?"

I hesitated for a moment. "Get out," I finally said.

"Get out and . . . ?"

"Stay out," I answered sulkily.

"So?"

"So, this is worse than The Bottom! I don't want to be here. It's hell!"

She sighed. "Kiddo, you know what hell looks like, and that school is not it."

"I don't care! I want to come home!"

"Listen, make it through one more week. Push through, graduate from being a plebe, and I'll send you something that will make it better, okay?"

I shook my head. "The upperclassmen take all my packages. They'll just steal whatever you send."

She laughed. "I promise you that they will not steal this."

I bit my lip. "Okay, fine. But I might still come home even after that."

"If you are still totally miserable after you graduate and get your gift, we can talk about you coming home."

I sniffed. "You promise?"

I could practically see her nodding. "Promise."

—

A week later I graduated. I made it out of plebe hell. And things immediately got better. I mean, I was still at the bottom of the barrel socially, and upperclassmen could still mess with me nonstop, and I still felt like my every step was monitored and tracked, but I knew I was out of the worst of it. But that didn't change my mind. Now that I had completed my end of the bargain, I was ready to tell Lezlie I still wanted to go home.

My heart squeezed whenever I thought about Viola Street. I imagined being back in the living room with my family, teasing and laughing. I thought about how good it would feel to return to the barn. I was certain that VF was never going to feel right to me. There was no way I was ever really going to fit in.

I walked down to the stables for practice, planning the speech in my mind that I was going to give to Lezlie when I called her later that night.

You promised me I could come home if I wanted to, I imagined myself saying.

I knew I'd have her there since Lezlie always kept her promises.

As I crossed the threshold into the barn, I thought about how maybe I could even convince her to come and get me that night. I was pretty sure I could be packed up and ready to go in no time at all. I might even make it home for dinner. Not like I needed to stay for any more mess hall slop.

I turned toward a stall and grabbed a halter, ready to pull out my usual mount. From behind me, a horse whinnied. My hand stilled halfway toward the stall door. Something clicked in my head.

Was that . . . ?

I heard the neigh again.

My heart started to pound. I knew that sound. It couldn't be anyone else.

I turned around slowly, afraid to say his name out loud.

Even louder. A trumpet of pure joy. He had seen me. And

finally, I saw him, at the end of the stables, his neck stretched out over the stall door, the little white star shining on his forehead, straining toward me and making excited little nickers.

I burst into tears and ran to him, not caring that Harris and Jones were watching, not caring that I looked like a big baby, wrapping my arms around Cholo's neck, burying my face in his mane.

Lezlie had sent me my pony.

She'd given me a reason to stay.

CHAPTER TWELVE

For three years before I came to Valley Forge, I had habitually skipped school.

I wasn't as bad as Bee or David had been, of course. I showed up just enough so that Lezlie would let me stay in the program, but I'd especially hated middle school and I thought it was an enormous waste of my time. Most kids in our neighborhood dropped out in their first couple of years of high school and I didn't see myself being much different except for the fact that I wanted to stay at the barn as long as I possibly could.

I was not a good student. I was the kind of kid who someone might ask what my favorite subject was and I'd answer, "Recess," and not even really mean that because even recess sucked at my school as far as I was concerned.

The schools in my neighborhood were overcrowded, run down, understaffed, and dangerous. I know that the teachers cared—I know that plenty of them were good people with good intentions—but their time and resources were so limited, the students needed so much, that I'm sure they were physically and emotionally depleted. They were in constant crisis mode. They just didn't have much left to give.

Practically all the students had access to guns, and the older we got, the more likely it became that a schoolyard grudge could turn into something much more serious. School shootings were common, but they were not the kind of school shootings that got national attention. The media never felt the need to breathlessly talk about every little Black kid who was killed. I can't count how many times I watched kids duck out at the end of the day and flat-out run home because they knew there was every chance that one of their schoolmates was going to meet them on the playground with a .45.

I shouldn't have been allowed to move up from grade to grade. I skipped so much school, and even when I managed to show up, I absorbed practically nothing. By the time I got to Valley Forge and started the eighth grade, I was at maybe a fourth- or fifth-grade level academically, but I didn't realize how truly behind I was until that first week of classes.

I was still a plebe, so at first I was relieved to be in the classroom because that meant that there were finally adults around and the hazing necessarily eased up. Our teacher was Mrs. Greene, a tiny, blond woman with a sweet smile. She was the kind of teacher who was so nice that even the worst kid felt like a real asshole if he gave her a hard time. Unlike my classes back in Philly, which had been full to overflowing, the class size at VF was small. Maybe eight to ten kids, total, and that meant there was no hiding or being overlooked.

Mrs. Greene was both my math and English teacher. She must have realized just how bad things were the first time she asked me to read out loud in class. We were studying *The Catcher in the Rye* (J. D. Salinger was a VF alumnus) and when I realized that students were going to be asked to read passages of it out loud, it was all I could do not to get up and run out of class.

"Kareem? Can you pick up where Michael left off?"

I bent over the page, hiding the flush of shame as I slowly and painfully began to read. "L-life is a . . . ga-game, boy. L-life is a . . . game that o-one plays . . . acc-c-ording to the . . . rules."

Someone laughed. A sneering giggle.

I looked up at Mrs. Greene. Hoping that was enough.

She gave me an encouraging smile. "Go on."

I looked back down at the page, miserable. "Yes, sir. I k-k-know it is. I . . . know it."

"Okay, Kareem, thank you. Eric, would you pick up where Kareem left off?"

I kept my eyes on my desk, hunched over as I listened to my classmate read smoothly and easily through the next couple of pages. I had never known what it was like to be embarrassed about the deficits in my education. I had never cared about schoolwork before. Nobody at my old school cared. There was no competition in those classrooms; even the smartest kids just sat there waiting for the day to end. But at VF, kids cared. They vied for the best grades. They noticed who was smart and who struggled, and they definitely noticed the guy who could hardly read.

Math was no better. We had a test that very first day. "Just to gauge where everyone is in their mathematical progress," Mrs. Greene said.

She handed back the tests, facedown, the next morning.

The classroom was small and the desks were close together, and I remember looking right and then left to see my classmates' scores: 87 percent on one side, 92 percent on the other, and then there was me: 53 percent. I had missed nearly half the answers.

"Kareem?" said Mrs. Greene. "I'd like to see you after class, please."

For the rest of the class, I couldn't follow a thing she was teaching us. Even if it had been at my level (which it most definitely was not) I wouldn't have been able to concentrate because I was fixated on the fact that I had to stay after class. I was so nervous, I honestly would have cheered if the ground had opened up and swallowed me whole.

"So," said Mrs. Greene after the classroom had emptied out. "You are obviously a bright boy, but I think you might need a little extra tutoring to catch up."

I looked away from her, embarrassed.

"You're not the only one, Kareem."

I shook my head. I knew that some kids who spoke English as a second language were getting help, but that was hardly an equivalent.

"Lots of people have to ask for help. There's absolutely nothing wrong with that. The only thing a student should feel bad about in my class is if they don't try their best."

That almost made me crack a smile. Mrs. Greene sounded like Lezlie when we were about to lose a game.

"Let's make a schedule. You can stay after class and we can work together. Let's say forty-five minutes each day, four days a week?"

I knit my brow. I couldn't imagine the teachers from my old school offering up four days of tutoring to anyone. Hell,

I could hardly imagine them giving me four minutes. By the end of the day, everyone just needed to get the hell out of that place and make it home in one piece.

—

That first year, it was all about getting through. In Philly, we have a saying: "Stayin' out the way." You say it when someone asks how you're doing. It's more honest than saying, "I'm good," or, "I'm fine." It means, you've got your head down and you're making it through whatever is currently being thrown at you. You're not causing a fuss. That's what I tried to do at VF. Stay out the way. Things were better after I graduated out of being a plebe, but I was still picked on and bullied constantly. Mrs. Greene tutored me and that helped a lot, but I was still always behind in all my subjects. I dreaded being called on in class, or worse yet, called up to the blackboard where I'd show everyone just how little I knew. I used to go back to the barracks at the end of the day and look at the stack of schoolbooks on my desk and cry, I was so overwhelmed by the amount of work. I was friendly with lots of kids, but I didn't feel particularly close to any one person. I had my teammates, and they respected me on the field, but even aside from all our obvious differences, they were seniors in high school, their parents were paying my tuition, and they had five years rank on me. It's not like we were going to hang around outside of the barn. We played hard, but the team didn't gel enough to get far. We got knocked out early that year.

I got a new roommate, Francisco from Ecuador. He was a really nice guy, but he had an addiction to Robitussin. He used to sit in the dark after reveille and drink it straight from the bottle until he started to hallucinate. I'd go to sleep each night listening to him mumbling to himself and trying to snatch invisible things out of the air with his hands.

—

"Arquetta died," said Gerb.

We were having our weekly catch-up call.

"Kareema's pony? Oh shit. How'd it happen?"

"Cancer, I guess. Lez said she had a tumor."

I sat down at my desk. "Damn. How is Kareema taking it? Can I talk to her?"

Gerb was quiet for a moment. "She's not here, Reem. I don't know where she is right now." I could hear him breathing. "She quit the barn."

I felt my chest tighten up. "What do you mean, she quit?"

"She hasn't really been showing up much ever since you left. She's been hooking school, so Lezlie wouldn't let her ride, and she got some new friends, you know? After Arquetta died, Lezlie tried to give her another horse to take care of—she even offered her Buddha—but Reema said no thanks. She said she was done with the barn."

I swallowed. "She hustling?"

"I don't know for sure. Probably. She's not around much anymore. She's different, Reem."

I was sick to my stomach. I couldn't stand to think about it. Shy, gentle Kareema living the life. "How about you?" I asked. It felt urgent. "You still riding at least?"

"Yeah, yeah, course I am. Lezlie says I'm getting real good, too."

I forced a deep breath. "You gotta keep playing, Gerb. You have to ride, okay?"

"I know. You don't have to worry about me. I like riding. Anyway, I'm probably better than you now. Pretty sure I could beat your ass."

I laughed. "I'd like to see you try."

—

After we hung up the phone, I thought about going home again. Finding Kareema and straightening things out. I played a little movie in my head about how maybe she'd be so happy I came back that she'd be willing to return to the barn and get back on the straight and narrow. Maybe she'd even want to play on the team. But deep down, I knew better. In her quiet way, Kareema was as headstrong as Bee and David, and she wasn't going to listen to me any more than they would have.

"Put your own oxygen mask on first, Kareem," Lezlie sighed when I talked to her later that week. "You can't control what Kareema does. Get your head down and take care of what you can take care of at Valley Forge, and maybe someday you'll be in the position where you can help your whole family out instead."

I knew she was right, but that didn't make me feel much better.

—

There were some legacy kids who were at Valley Forge because it was a family tradition, and there were some kids who were real smart or talented and were there on academic or sports scholarships like me, but the remaining population of the campus was rich fuckups and near juvenile delinquents. The first question you asked when you met someone was, "What did you do to get sent here?" Bad grades. Not being

the kid their parents wanted. Stealing. Lying. Fighting. Dis-
obedience. This was a last-chance sort of place. Which isn't to
say it didn't help some of us. Sometimes a last chance becomes
a new beginning. But it was hard to think that way when every moment of every day felt like a struggle to do things right.

Riding helped, of course. I was on horseback four days a
week, practicing with my teammates, laying my hands on the
ponies. Training on high-end horses was a revelation. I'd had
the chance to ride real polo ponies when we played games, of
course, but until I had access to the VF string, I didn't realize just how much harder I'd had to work riding a horse like
Buck on the day to day. I could learn so much faster when I
wasn't constantly fighting against my pony's bad habits.

There were some great horses in that stable, and a couple that I really loved, but of course, it was Cholo who really helped me get through things. He was thriving in the
VF stables. He was lean and muscled and getting faster and
more precise every time I rode him, and he kept that sweet,
easygoing nature that made him so fun to train. He was nervous with the other horses, though, sometimes nipping and
starting things up when they were turned out together, like
he knew they weren't his kind. I couldn't help thinking that
Cholo and I were the same, a couple of ghetto kids surrounded
by the elite who'd had everything just handed to them from
the very beginning of their lives. We had slipped into this
place because of our talent, but we were both still uneasy and
couldn't help feeling like we didn't really belong.

—

In 1984, an organization called Mural Arts Philadelphia was
established to help fight against urban blight and graffiti. Some

extremely talented artists and a bunch of volunteers came together to start painting murals on the sides of buildings in low-income neighborhoods. The art was meant to reflect the local culture and heroes. They did a three-story version of Dr. J wearing glasses and a suit. They did an eight-story portrait of local Black kids interspersed with white women in Victorian gowns and Greek heroes. There was even a big piece in our neighborhood dedicated to the Black Cowboys.

These murals became famous worldwide. Prince Charles and his wife Camilla came to tour them; everybody knew about them. So when Lezlie called me at VF, all excited, to let me know that they wanted to do a painting dedicated to Work to Ride and polo, and that the artist wanted to base two of his models on me and Bee, I knew it was a big deal.

Trouble started before the mural was even finished. It was being painted literally ten blocks from our house on Viola Street, but when it became clear what the subject matter was, a lot of people in The Bottom thought it was a joke, that they were being mocked. What the hell were a bunch of Black kids from the hood doing dressed up like polo players? They'd never heard of Work to Ride, they didn't know there were kids in our neighborhood playing and excelling at polo, and the few that did know, like some of the Black Cowboys, didn't necessarily like or trust Lezlie. They didn't like a white woman getting all this publicity, and they complained that her focus was on getting kids out, instead of finding a way to have us stay and help to make things better at home.

"I need you this Saturday, Kareem," said Lezlie. "I'll request a day pass for you to come. The mural is done but people are still grumbling. We need to show them who we are."

It wasn't a big event. Lezlie brought over some of our

easier ponies to offer rides to neighborhood kids. There were trays of free food and a cooler of drinks. Some clumsy autumn decorations were wrapped around the small fence that surrounded the grass in front of the mural to make things feel a little more like a party. The artist was there and gave a speech about how he was so proud to paint us and impressed by how much we'd accomplished. Lezlie talked a little about Work to Ride and invited people to come visit our barn. There were kids from Work to Ride running around and leading the horses, some parents from the program, some people from the neighborhood, some curious kids poking around who had been attracted by the food and pony rides.

Gerb and I sat on the fence in the weak sunlight and watched as little kids were put on ponies, legs dangling, and led around the yard. I felt easy for the first time in weeks. It was comfortable to be back in the neighborhood, to be surrounded by people I knew and recognized.

"I thought Bee or Reema might show," I said.

Gerb shot me an incredulous look. "You did?"

I shrugged. "That's Bee up there on the wall, isn't it?"

Gerb shook his head. "He seen it already."

"I guess Mom couldn't make it, either," I said. "I thought maybe she'd bring Washika."

Gerb frowned. "Mom's not feeling good right now."

I knew what that was code for. She was using again. I had suspected as much. Lately she'd sounded real down anytime she called me at school.

"What about Washika? She okay?"

Gerb nodded. "Yeah, we got people. Don't worry."

I was quiet for a moment, watching Lezlie laugh with one of the kids from the barn.

I took a deep breath. "I don't have to go back, you know. I could quit school and stay home and help."

Gerb kept his eyes on the ponies. "Naw," he finally said. He sounded kind of mad. "How's that gonna change anything?"

"It's a lot for you to manage," I said. "You're just a kid."

Gerb laughed. "*You're* just a kid, Reem."

"Yeah, but—"

Gerb hopped down from the fence and finally looked at me. "You know the rule; if you get out, stay out. You come back, you just gonna end up like Reema and Bee and David."

He didn't wait for me to answer. Just turned and walked away, heading for the ponies, his narrow little shoulders squared and tense.

I was supposed to be helping with the horses and mingling with the guests, but I stayed on that fence for a long time, just watching the pony rides and looking at that big mural: me and Bee in helmets and jerseys, riding ponies that looked a lot like Cholo, our mallets caught midswing, four stories high.

After I returned to Valley Forge that night, I lay in bed after reveille, listening to Francisco bump around the room, swigging cough syrup and mumbling softly to himself. I felt helpless. My family was falling apart.

I understood that Gerb and Lezlie were right. I knew that I wouldn't be any real help to anybody if I dropped out, but at the same time, it felt all wrong to be so far from them, for me to be safely tucked away while they were still in danger.

That was the problem with *get out and don't come back*. There were always those that you had to leave behind.

CHAPTER THIRTEEN

Lezlie was determined to keep me out of Philly, so in the summer between eighth and ninth grades, she arranged for me to go in live with the Gomez family in Lakeville, Connecticut. They were friends of Lezlie's, and the father, Mark, was a farrier. They also raised and trained polo ponies.

They were good people. They taught me a lot and made me feel welcome. My only job that summer was to ride green horses. Every morning I would wake up and walk through the barnyard, out to the stables, saddle up whatever pony I was working with, and think, *I could do this forever*. After a year of struggling with academics, and hewing to the rules, and eating terrible food, and having my every step and breath dictated, a summer in the country training ponies and playing polo was exactly what I needed. Every time I helped to gentle a young horse, I felt like I shook off a little more of the Valley Forge robot I had become. Nobody on that farm was asking me to conform or march or say, "Yes, sir!" "No, sir!" or do anything except climb into the saddle and do what I already loved to do.

When the summer was over and it was time to return to school, I was miserable. I wished with all my heart that I could stay in Connecticut and train horses for the rest of my life. I never wanted to think about military school again. Of course, that was not an option.

Jones and Harris had graduated, so there was a new polo team that year. Two more seniors, Jake Langtry from Maryland and Luis Rojas from Colombia, and me. They were good players, but I was better than them, and we all knew it. I wasn't going to be captain because I was still too young, but I tried very hard to ignore that fact and run the field and call the shots anyway. I thought a lot about how, when Bee was in charge, Andy and I had just stood back and let him play. I didn't understand why Langtry and Rojas weren't giving me the same respect. I was certain that I could win singlehandedly, just like Bee used to do, if they would just make the space and let me play through. Needless to say, I was kind of a shit teammate.

———

My summer on the farm in Connecticut made it especially hard to transition back to military life. I was no longer a plebe (second-year cadets were called "old men" and also, less affectionately, "shit bags"), so things didn't feel as violent or overwhelming as they'd been the year before, but at least in my first year there had been some novelty in my days. I might have suffered, but I was never bored. I knew exactly what I was facing in my second year, and I knew that it would be a terrible slog. I wasn't senior enough to enjoy the privileges the ranked cadets would have, and at the same time, I was expected to scrupulously follow every tiny rule since I was already trained. I hated it. I especially despised the way so many of the rules seemed so arbitrary, just there to make our lives harder.

Sometimes I thought about those days when I was only a visitor at this school, when Bee and Andy and I had played against them, and how the cadets had told us story after story about trying to escape, beat the system, find some semblance of a normal, non-VF life. At the time, I'd just laughed. I thought those stories were hilarious exaggerations, but now, when I replayed them back in my mind, I wished I had listened closer and learned. They weren't tall tales; they were warnings.

—

A couple weeks into the semester, our team was invited to play a game at a polo club about an hour north of the school. It wasn't an official, on-the-roster game, but we figured it was close enough. The school disagreed; when we requested the day pass we'd need to go, we were denied.

To my thirteen-year-old mind, this denial seemed the same as withholding candy from us as plebes—mean and punishing for no particular reason. This made me reckless.

"They won't even notice we're gone," I said to Langtry and Rojas. "No one ever checks the stables."

We were just finishing up our morning practice and I was needling my teammates as we put our ponies away. We all wanted to go to the game, but Rojas and Langtry weren't sold on the idea of leaving school without permission.

"What's the worst that could happen if we did it?" I said as I sprayed my pony down in the shower stall.

"We could get thrown in front of the academic board and get a tour," said Langtry.

"So what?" I said. "So we get a tour."

Rojas looked at me, amused. "Have you ever had a tour, Rosser?"

I shrugged. "No, but they don't seem like that big a deal."

Rojas and Langtry laughed.

"I almost want to go to this game just so you can get a tour and then eat those words," said Langtry.

"Great!" I dragged the scraper over my horse's pelt, squeezing off the excess water. "Let's do it, then!"

I watched them exchange a look.

"All right," said Rojas. "I'm in. But if we get caught, I'm definitely going to say that it was Rosser's idea."

I whooped. "Yes! You'll drive, right, Langtry?" Langtry had a very nice car.

He slowly shook his head. "Fine. But you better hope they don't notice we're gone. You're not going to like it if you get caught, Rosser."

I shrugged them off. In my mind, I was still Summer Kareem. And Summer Kareem was allowed to have fun and do as he liked. I was certain we'd get away with it.

I don't remember much about the game or the polo club. I don't even remember if we won or lost, but what I do remember is that by the time we got back, they had already figured out where we had gone.

My tac officer (what might be called a dorm dad at other schools) was waiting for me outside my room. I was immediately brought to another building and presented to a panel of staff members and high-ranking cadets. They played dumb with me at first. They wanted to see if I would cop to where we'd been, or lie. Unfortunately, I lied. I insisted that I'd been at the stables the whole day.

They said that they had called down to the stables looking for me, and nobody had answered.

"That's so weird," I said, trying my best to look innocent. "Must be something wrong with the phone because I never heard it ring and like I said, I was there all day."

There was silence in the room as I brazenly met everyone's eyes, sure that I could fake my way out of this mess.

"All right," one of them finally said. "Get out, Cadet. Go back to your barracks. We're going to talk to your teammates."

I walked back to the barracks feeling like I'd dodged a bullet. I was so dumb that I was sure I'd gotten away with it, and even though Rojas and Langtry had teased about blaming me for everything, I didn't think they would spill.

But the staff already knew what we'd done, so my teammates didn't have to spill anything, and unlike me, when questioned directly, they weren't stupid enough to lie. I was called back within the hour.

This time they didn't bother waiting to see what I had to say. They started yelling at me the moment I came through the door. I was being charged for going AWOL and for lying, which meant double punishment. I would be restricted to the campus for a month and given a double dose of tours.

A tour was the formalized method of punishment at VF.

Every tour was the equivalent of an hour, and if you were given a month of tours, it meant that not only did you lose all your off-campus privileges, but any moment of free time you might have had on-campus would now be taken up with fulfillment of your punishment.

I was told to report to the parade grounds at 6:00 A.M. sharp the next morning to start my tour.

Of course, I'd seen kids being punished before, and I'd heard stories about how much it sucked, but I was in no way prepared when I showed up, shivering in the damp morning air, and a fifty-pound World War II rifle full of lead was shoved into my hands.

"Now march in a square until I tell you you're done, you shit bag!" ordered my squad leader. He was pissed off that he had to spend his morning supervising me.

I hefted the gun up onto my shoulder. It weighed about twice what my usual rifle did. My boots sank into the muddy ground with every step I took.

I marched for three hours. I marched until the gun drilled into my shoulder blade and my arms went numb and my knees felt like they were about to give out from under me. Every time I dragged a little or tried to slow down, my squad leader started screaming and promising to add more time to the punishment. By the time I was done, my arms and legs were shaking so hard, I thought I might collapse. Summer Kareem was long gone.

"Did you enjoy that, Rosser?" asked my squad leader. He didn't sound mean anymore, just conversational.

"No, sir!" I answered.

He shrugged and took the gun from my trembling hands.

"Too bad, since you got another month ahead of you with this little baby." He stroked the rifle like it was a kitten.

—

When you are found guilty at a disciplinary board (or two boards, in my case) you are not only restricted to campus, you are also removed from whatever extracurriculars you might be involved with. I was taken off the polo team. Since Langtry and Rojas were being punished, too, this meant that there was no polo team at all. And since all of my free time was being sucked up by endlessly marching in a square carrying an antique fifty-pound rifle, I wasn't even allowed to set foot in the stables for a month.

It had been years since I'd gone more than a few days without horses. There had been plenty of times when I couldn't actually ride. Because Work to Ride didn't have an indoor arena, basically all lessons and games stopped at the barn right after the first snowfall of the winter, but I still could groom and feed and just be around the barn and ponies when I needed them. It wasn't until they were taken away from me entirely that I realized how much I had come to depend on them for my day-to-day well-being.

Every night I'd lie awake, feeling the rhythm of the march throb relentlessly in my limbs, my head gripped in a dull whirl, thinking about how much I hated school, how stupid the rules were, how I wished I was still on the farm in Connecticut or back home in the barn. The school had grooms taking care of the horses, but I worried about Cholo missing me. He wouldn't understand why I had disappeared. Then my anxiety would ramp up even more and I'd start worrying about my family and Lezlie and feeling guilty for leaving them and wondering if everyone was okay. By morning, I was exhausted, and it didn't help that I still had more fruitless hours of marching ahead of me.

Maybe that's why, at the end of that month, practically on my last day of probation, I finally snapped.

I was not the biggest kid on campus. Like all the boys in my family, I hit puberty kind of late. At fourteen, I was not particularly tall or built yet. Years of working in a barn had left me wiry and strong, but if you didn't know that, you might have looked at me and just seen a scrawny little kid. That, plus my natural anxiety and tendency toward shyness, made me an easy mark for bullies, and there were plenty of bullies at VF. A military school attracts a lot of kids who are broken. Kids who are broken are often cruel. The culture of the school, the hazing and the plebe system, and the fact that the older kids were put in charge of the younger, more vulnerable ones, all contributed to a place where bullying felt like second nature. It was baked into the cake, so to speak.

I wasn't helpless. I'd grown up with three brothers (and Kareema, who could hold her own when she needed to). I was used to teasing and wrestling and the occasional full-on brawl. But I'd also grown up in a place where you learned early on to be very careful about picking your battles, because anyone could have a gun, and a lot of people didn't think twice about using it. There was no such thing as a harmless fight in The Bottom. So when kids came after me at VF, I kept my head down and tolerated it. They'd call me names or push me around and try to get me to react, but I found that if I just shut up and took it instead of fighting back, they usually got bored and it ended pretty fast.

But then there was Kurt Heinz. He was the same grade as me, but big and mean, with a jutting jaw and pale blue eyes, and for some reason, it was his pet project to make me miserable every time he saw me. I'd dodged him on the regular all through my first year, but he had come back even harder during my second.

We were in the mess, lining up to collect our dinner at the steam tables, when he brushed past me in line, knocking me aside with his shoulder, and hissing, "Get the fuck out of my way, you porch monkey."

I felt the blood rush to my face as every muscle in my body went tense. He had said some awful things in the past, but this was the first time he'd taken it to this place.

"What did you just say to me?" I was surprised by just how calm my voice sounded.

He turned and met my eyes, a big, ugly smile on his face.

"I said, get the fuck out of my way, nigger."

That was it. I was done. I wanted to launch myself straight for his throat, but I wasn't totally stupid—the mess was full of staff members.

"Okay. You want to go like that?" I said. "Let's go, then. Meet me back in my room." And I turned and walked out of the mess.

He followed right behind me, and he brought friends. At least fifteen other kids crowded into my room behind him, peering over each other's shoulders and trickling out into the hall.

I didn't care. I was so sick of this. After all this time being targeted and picked on and bullied day after day, I was filled with the kind of rage that was just waiting for the right person to say the wrong thing at the perfect time.

Heinz entered the room slowly, still smiling, his chest stuck out and a mean look in his eyes. I'd seen him beat other kids. He always picked cadets who were smaller than him, and he always went harder than he had to.

He stepped up close to me. I could smell his breath. "So you wanna go?" he said. He pushed at my shoulder, shoving me backward. "Let's go, then, nigger!"

I didn't fight a lot. I was the kid who normally avoided conflict, who preferred to stand back and watch instead of getting into it. Violence was not my thing. But for five years, I'd been swinging a mallet from horseback. I'd been hitting balls that went singing through the air at a hundred miles per hour. I'd been carrying saddles and stacking hay bales and shoveling shit. So when I used that same arm to haul back and then smash Heinz right in his ugly, smirking face, there was strength there that no one but me knew I had.

His nose shattered into splinters. I felt it explode under my knuckles, crunching like a sack of gravel. I saw an arc of blood spray through the air, felt the warmth as it hit my shirt and then the floor. Then I felt an excruciating pain in my hand. I had cracked my own thumb.

Heinz buried his face in his hands and doubled over without ever taking a swing.

"Fuck!" he screamed as blood pumped through his fingers. His voice sounded thick and adenoidal. "Fuck! You fucking broke my nose!"

The crowd howled as one.

"Oh man! Oh shit!"

"He really did it!"

"The kid took you down, Heinz!"

Heinz looked up at me. "You fucking asshole, Rosser!" I could tell he was trying to be tough, but his voice sounded mealy and tearful, like a little kid with a skinned knee.

My hand was throbbing, but I held my fist up again as I took a step closer to him. "You want more?"

Heinz scuttled backward, almost falling on his ass, and the crowd burst into laughter. That's when I won the fight for sure. Blood was dripping on the floor, he was whimpering in pain, everyone was laughing, but I still imagined hitting him again and again until his piggy little eyes swelled shut, until his face was a bloody pulp. I imagined how good it would feel. I stepped forward, gearing up, but before I could take another swing, my tac officer was in the room, taking in the gory scene.

"What the hell, Cadet?" he roared as he grabbed me by the collar and lifted me backward. "Okay, you two, come with me."

———

I had to wait a week to find out what my sentence would be, but since it was my third board in a month's time, I was pretty sure I was going to be expelled. I called Lezlie, hoping for a sympathetic ear. The school had already contacted her to let her know what happened, but she listened patiently as I described my end of the story.

"Well," she finally said, with a little chuckle, "I think I might have broken his nose, too."

"Right?" I said. "It's not fair! I didn't do anything wrong!"

"Oh, I didn't say that. You definitely messed up, Kareem."

"But—"

"Now, I'm not saying you were wrong to stand up to that racist little jerk—"

"He wasn't little."

She laughed again. "Fine. But if you get kicked out, it's not going to be because you got into this fight. It's going to be that you got into this fight on top of the fact that you went AWOL and then lied about it."

"But we only left campus because we had a game! I thought you, of all people, would understand!"

Her voice grew colder. "Seriously? Being on that team is a privilege, not a right. How many times did I ban you from playing when you messed up here?"

"A few times, I guess," I admitted.

"I'd say more than a few, Kareem."

"This place sucks," I said sulkily. "I hope I do get kicked out."

Lezlie was quiet for a moment. Then I heard her sigh. "And what will you do then?"

I frowned, surprised. "What do you mean?"

"I mean, if you get kicked out, what's next? What will you do after that?"

"I'll come home," I said. "Back to the barn."

"You can't live in the barn, Kareem. And you can't be part of Work to Ride if you're not in school. Are you planning to go back to the school here? Show up to classes and get good grades?"

I hesitated. "I mean, sure. Yeah."

"You sure weren't doing that before you left for Valley Forge."

"But Lez—" I whined.

She cut me off. "Did you hear that David got his sentence for dealing?"

I felt the breath go out of me. I knew his trial had been this week but I hadn't had a chance to talk to anyone about it yet.

"Six years."

I felt sick to my stomach. "Oh no," I whispered.

"Listen to me, kiddo." Her voice sounded tired. "If they let you stay, and I hope they do, you gotta pull it together and figure out how to make this work. You are a smart kid, but you sure aren't acting like one. You have been given a chance to change your life, and right now, you are just throwing that chance away."

—

They let me stay.

Heinz and I were each sentenced to three months of tours. By now, I understood exactly what that meant: no time off campus, no privileges, more forced marching, and no horses from the end of September until the end of January.

I thought long and hard about what Lezlie had said to me. There were kids all around me every day trying to beat the system, and I never saw one succeed. They were either caught and punished, or they were thrown out of the school. I didn't want to be one those kids anymore. Like David, I had been so convinced that I was special, that I could beat the system, but that idea was sending me down the same road; I was either going to get punished, or I was going to get thrown away.

Neither felt acceptable to me anymore.

Though I'm sure my older brothers might roll their eyes

at me for saying so, those tours were the closest thing I ever experienced to prison. For four months, I was trapped and miserable and exhausted. My time was never my own, there was not the smallest spark of joy or comfort in my life, and there were no horses.

Six years, I'd remind myself as I was marching through the sleet.

I decided I didn't want to leave.

Word got around fast about the fight, and things started to change for me after that. I never had another kid bully me again, and for years after, whenever Heinz would start to lose his shit at anyone else, his friends would laugh and say, "You better chill out before we go get Rosser, man!"

I also started doing better academically because if I was in class studying with Mrs. Greene, that meant I wasn't outside in the snow marching with a fifty-pound rifle; it was the first time in my life that I actively chose to be in a classroom. I finally realized that the only way to get anything at the school was to earn it. If I did well, worked hard, and stuck to the rules, I would be invited back into Leadership Detail and be given seniority. Seniority meant privilege. Privilege meant polo. Polo meant freedom. It sounded crazy, but I finally figured out that I had to comply to be allowed the room to be myself.

It's not that they broke me, it's more like I just realized that I didn't need to make everything so damned hard. My habit of standing back and watching started to pay off. I learned to code-switch. I became a chameleon. I could get along with anyone. I charmed the staff. I made a point of hanging around with the ranked cadets. I shined my shoes and kept my uniform pressed and said, "No, sir!" and "Yes, sir!"

with the right amount of respect. What I'd learned in those Hamptons mansions came back to me; appearances mattered, the little niceties set you apart, fitting in made people want to help you succeed.

—

I finally realized that it had never been about beating the system; it was all about figuring out how to play the game.

CHAPTER FOURTEEN

It looked like I was going to finish off the year on a high point. I was done with my tours, my grades were much better, and there hadn't been any more incidents since I broke Heinz's nose. I was not only playing polo, but soccer, tennis, and baseball, too. I was well on my way to becoming a model cadet.

I had access to the ponies again but our team came back into the season late, with very little time to practice, and it showed. We had zero chance of even placing in the regionals, never mind making the nationals, but honestly, I didn't care. After being away for so long, I played like a starving man who had just been seated in front of a banquet; I couldn't get enough of the game.

As summer quickly approached, I was already looking forward to the next year. I thought I had a pretty good shot at being invited back into Leadership Detail, which meant that I'd be given both more responsibility and more freedom.

I was also pretty sure I'd be appointed captain of the polo team, and I looked forward to having the chance to finally shape us into being championship players.

So when I first started hearing rumors about financial issues at the academy and certain programs being cut, I didn't pay them much mind. The athletic program was one of the untouchable cornerstones of the school. They had a rabid alumni fan base; I was certain that there was no way they were going to mess with that kind of VF tradition. What I didn't take into account was that, even at an elite prep school like Valley Forge, polo was still mostly seen as an overindulgent, niche sport—croquet on horseback for the rich.

VF had football, basketball, soccer, baseball, tennis, lacrosse, swimming, and track and field. The place was crawling with student athletes, and the good ones were pretty much universally admired. Because I was Black and played polo, people were maybe a little more interested in me than they were in my white teammates, but it wasn't like I was a quarterback or a point guard. I was more freak than star. Nobody was tailgating our games or painting their faces to cheer us on. Sometimes I liked to imagine what it would have been like to live someplace like Argentina, where polo is a sport of the people, recognized for the dangerous, difficult game it really is, instead of being seen as a rich man's pastime. I wondered what it would have been like to have been as adored as NFL or NBA stars. To have been seen as a skilled athlete rather than a curiosity.

My scholarship was not guaranteed. Funds for it had to be found and renewed year to year. Since the polo kids and families who had initially recruited me and paid for my first year had all graduated and moved on, I knew that we'd have to find new donors to keep me on at the school. We had already done this once between my eighth and ninth grade years, but I had been reassured by Lezlie and the VF horsemanship director that other families in the polo program would certainly step forward to help out, so I wasn't worried about that, either.

With everything I'd gone through that year, and the solid place where I had ended up, it just never occurred to me that something as foundational as the reason I was at the school in the first place could ever be threatened.

—

We heard about the horsemanship director being fired about a week before graduation. It was a shock, but at first I didn't understand what, exactly, that meant for our program. When the team was called into the coach's office, I was expecting to hear that we'd be tightening our belt; I'd imagined there might be more cuts to the barn—fewer ponies, no new equipment, maybe a smaller traveling budget. This didn't faze me much. I was used to making do and doing without. But as soon as I saw our coach's face, I knew it was worse than I'd expected.

"I'm so sorry, boys. As of next year, the school will no longer be participating in polo in any way. They will be selling off the ponies over the summer. They just don't feel that they can justify supporting such an expensive program."

It was a punch to the gut. I'd always understood that I was brought to the school to make the team better, but it was only after they told me that they were shutting it down that it occurred to me that maybe I'd been recruited with the hope that I'd save the program altogether. I knew that the polo team had been on the chopping block before—that the players and their families had fought to keep it in years past—but up until that moment, I don't think I'd understood that it had truly been in jeopardy. I mean, I knew why it was being cut. It made sense. There was probably no sport that was more expensive than the one built around a bunch of six-figure, thoroughbred horses. The school might have justified the cost if we were winning and creating good press, but the team had not had a championship for many years.

The night after we were told that the program was cut, I sat in my dorm room and tortured myself, wondering if I had managed to deliver a trophy or two, maybe we would have been safe.

Lezlie called me as soon as she heard the news. She knew I'd be spinning out. She told me not to worry, that she was in touch with the head of the school and that he had assured her, polo or no polo, they wanted to find a way for me stay on.

"We'll figure this out, kiddo. In the meantime, you'll go back to the Gomez farm for the summer, just like we planned. And actually, I was going to surprise you with this, but I'll tell you now since you need a little cheering up—they've invited Gerb out for the summer as well."

"That's great," I said, trying to sound enthusiastic.

I was glad that the head of the school was helping, but I didn't have much hope. Sure, I had been doing my best to shape up as a cadet, but without polo, it was hard to understand why VF would even bother with me. I decided that if things fell apart, I would ask the Gomez family if they would be willing to hire me on a permanent basis.

—

When I first arrived at the farm, I tried to do as Lezlie instructed and put it all out of my mind. Lakeville was as green and bucolic as ever, and working with young horses every day required that I be completely in the moment. When you're training, your horses are, by definition, unpredictable. If you ride when you're distracted or tired, if you let your mind wander, if you start thinking about lunch instead of the work you're doing, you could end up on the ground, or worse yet, under your horse. Every horse farm has a horror story about a leg broken in five places or a rider being dragged, or much, much worse. Every trainer has scars to show off, stories to tell. It was always a little bit amazing to me that I could be fearful of so many things in my life, but riding horses and playing polo, both extremely dangerous pastimes, were things I couldn't live without. I enjoyed training almost as much as I loved playing. They scratched the same emotional spot for me—having command over a massive, thousand-pound animal when very few other things in my life were in my control.

Still, even training colts couldn't completely drive away the anxiety I felt about the upcoming school year. I had been brought to the school for a reason, and now the reason was gone. I did my best to keep my worries on lockdown, saving the worst of them for late at night, when my racing thoughts and bad dreams woke me up with a violent jolt and shudder.

Gerb arrived a few days after I did, wide eyed and excited. He'd never really been outside of Philly before, and because Lezlie had been relentless about keeping me from returning home for any longer than a week or so at a time, it had been almost two years since he and I'd had the chance to spend any real time together.

I was happy to show him around the farm, assuming a casual expertise as if I owned the place. I loved watching his mouth drop open when he saw the beautiful stables and all the pro-level ponies. It reminded me of the time I'd visited Bee in Texas.

Gerb and I talked on the phone almost every week while I was at school, but seeing him in person made me realize how much he'd changed. My twelve-year-old brother seemed older than he was, mature beyond his years. He held his shoulders as if he was a little bit burdened. I worried about what he had been forced to carry while I was gone.

"Everything okay at home?" I asked him as we walked through the barn. "How's Mom? Washika getting taken care of?"

He nodded. "Mom's good. Been going to NA. Washika's never out of her sight these days. I swear, Mom babies her like she never babied the rest of us."

"And Reema? She coming around?"

He reached over and stroked a pony's nose. "Naw. She's gone more than ever."

I imagined how it must feel for him, being one of the last ones left at home. Being the only one left who was responsible for Washika when my mom was using.

"Gerb, you know if things ever get out of hand, you can always call me. Lezlie can get me a pass if you need me to be home."

He half smiled. "I know. Honestly, though, Mom's doing pretty good these days. It hasn't been bad."

—

Gerb's given name was actually Daymar, but we started calling him Gerb when he was an infant because my mom said that when he smiled, he was cuter than the Gerber baby.

1) David riding at Work to Ride, August 2000.

(Lezlie Hiner)

2) Mecca and Buddha, October 2002.

(Lezlie Hiner)

3) Andy, Kareem, and Bee at the Northeast Regional Tournament, March 2006.
(Lezlie Hiner)

4) Kareem and Jabarr playing at the Eldorado Polo Club in Indio, California, April 2006.
(Lezlie Hiner)

5) Kareem's first day at Valley Forge, August 2007.

(Lezlie Hiner)

6) Drea, Kareem, and Daymar before regionals, April 2009.

(Lezlie Hiner)

7) Daymar's first day at Valley Forge, August 2009.
(Lezlie Hiner)

8) Tummy, 2009.
(Lezlie Hiner)

9) & 10) The stables, July 2010.

(Lezlie Hiner)

11) Kareem in the 2011 National Interscholastic finals, March 2011.
(Lezlie Hiner)

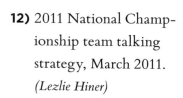

12) 2011 National Championship team talking strategy, March 2011.
(Lezlie Hiner)

13) 2011 National Championship team and Lezlie, March 2011.
(Lezlie Hiner)

14) Kareem graduating from Valley Forge, May 2011.
(Lezlie Hiner)

15) Cholo, July 2011.

(Lezlie Hiner)

16) Lazette and children, March 2013.

(Photo courtesy of the author)

My little brother was brave, funny, and charming like David and Bee, and he felt things deeply like me and Kareema, but he had a temper that was all his own. When he felt something was unfair, his rage was instant and molten. This had been true since he was tiny baby. We all used to stand around and watch in awe when he flew into a temper tantrum. He'd fling his little body to the ground and batter his feet and fists on the floor and scream so loud my ears would ring. There was truly no way to end it until he was through it. The only thing to do was clear the way around him so he didn't hurt himself or anyone else, and then just wait until he had sobbed himself out.

Luckily there was nothing to rage against at the farm. It was everything The Bottom was not: beautiful, quiet, clean, safe, and green. We were treated like family, given a nice room to share, invited to sit down at all the family meals, and basically offered run of their home. Every morning we'd get up at dawn, yawning and stretching as we got dressed and brushed our teeth and washed our faces. We'd have a quick breakfast with the family and then we'd head straight out to the barn where the ponies were waiting for us.

Summers in Connecticut start out cool in the mornings. The barn was especially chilly when we first walked in, but we warmed up quick, hauling the water buckets and throwing in flakes of hay and bowls of grain for the morning meal. By the time the last pony was fed, the first ones would be done eating, so we'd slide on their halters and lead them out into the fields, being careful to remember which ponies got turned out together and which ones needed to be kept apart. Once all the horses were out of the barn, we'd go back in and start shoveling shit and cleaning stalls, something we had mastered under Lezlie. I had grown to love the way a nice even line of shavings signified a stall was well cleaned, the way the wooden tack trunks were placed outside each stall, the fact that every horse had an embossed metal name plate attached to their door. There was an order to that barn that deeply appealed to me. I liked the way that everything had its place. Every pitchfork and broom was hung just so, every bucket was cleaned and stacked in its proper corner. I loved the tack room best of all, with its gleaming saddles set upon their stands, the braided bridles hanging from their hooks on the wall, the long line of helmets arranged upon the shelf, shiny pairs of boots running the length of one side, and an entire wall of multicolored ribbons—blue, red, yellow, white—all on display to be admired. There was order, abundance, and possibility all in one small room.

Once we were done cleaning, Gerb and I would go out and catch the ponies we'd been assigned to that day. Gerb usually got the one who needed less work, and I got the greener pony. We'd bring them in, groom and tack them up, and then take them out into the ring—or into the indoor if it was raining—and start our day's work. Later on, we'd take a break for lunch and then switch out ponies for the rest of the afternoon.

Riding with my brother alongside me felt like things were right with the world again. I'd enjoyed training with my teammates at school, but we were only tight on the field; I was still too young and unranked for them to spend any real time with me, and when I rode with them, I always felt like I had something to prove. Working and riding with Gerb, on the other hand, was nothing but a pleasure; we teased and trash-talked each other, keeping up a running dialogue as we

cleaned stalls and groomed ponies. We trained our horses together, sometimes just getting in the saddle and taking them
around the ring to teach them the basics, sometimes taking
them out to the polo field if the ponies were advanced enough.

—

The first time Gerb and I had a chance to ride a couple chukkers together, I was delighted to see how far he had come.

"Big man!" I yelled as he reached over and managed to
pluck the ball from my control. "Was that luck or did you
finally learn how to play?"

Gerb shook his head beneath his helmet. "Naw, bro!
Pretty sure you're just getting old and slow!" He laughed as
he grabbed his stick with both hands and sent the ball flying
down the field.

—

At night, after we finished riding and put the ponies up, we'd
stand at the edge of the fields and smell the earth cooling down
around us. We'd listen to frogs sing, watch the fireflies float in
the tall grass, tilt our faces up and see dozens of bats silhouetted
against the dusky sky, making curves and swoops through the
air as the stars blinked awake, one by one.

—

Word got around, and pretty soon people started to show up
to watch us play and invite us to their clubs and farms. I'd experienced something like this kind of attention when I used to
ride with Bee, but this was new for Gerb. He loved it. Putting
him in front an audience made him up his game. He was still
small for his age, and he had to compensate for his size by using

two hands to swing the mallet, but he rode like a bat out of hell to make up for it.

A friend of the Gomez family named Dennis Fitzpatrick invited us to come play on his farm. We spent a morning on his incredible ponies, playing stick and ball on his perfectly manicured field, having a blast. Afterward, he sat down with us at lunch and asked us about ourselves. Sometimes when this happened, I felt like I was on display, being examined as some sort of curiosity; come see the Black kid who plays the white man's sport. It was one of the things that drove me to be better. If white people were going to watch us play, I wasn't going to give them the satisfaction of failing. But Dennis didn't make me feel that way; he seemed genuinely interested in both me and Gerb. He didn't just ask questions, he told us stories about his own life and family, too. He honestly seemed to enjoy our company. Near the end of the meal, when he found out that I was at Valley Forge but Gerb was still attending public school in Philly, he spontaneously offered to pay for Gerb to attend VF as well.

It was a little strange when things like that happened. On one hand, it felt like pure luck, being in the right place at the right time; but on the other hand, there was usually a *reason* we were in the right place at the right time. You can call it talent or hard work or, more accurately, both. Gerb was in Connecticut that summer because I had been invited back after doing a good job working there the year before. Lezlie had been able to get me the job in the first place because she knew that, even at thirteen, I had the tenacity and skill set to help train horses. Dennis Fitzpatrick invited us to play on his field because he'd heard we were good polo players, but he offered to sponsor Gerb because when he sat down and talked with him, he saw a nice kid who deserved a chance.

As I had found out the hard way when the VF polo program folded, there were often strings attached to this kind of generosity, and they didn't always make themselves plain until after you had accepted it. But Dennis Fitzpatrick was one of the few people we met who truly just saw a deserving kid who needed a leg up, and had the means and the heart to give it to him. He'd be a friend to Gerb for years to come.

Gerb and I went back to the farm that night chattering and excited about the idea that we could go to school together. I warned him that the first six weeks would be hell (but I was privately already thinking about how I could make the plebe system a little easier on him than it had been on me) and we talked about the fact that there was no polo team for us to play on, no horses for us to be around, but with the two of us at school together, the idea that we wouldn't have access to ponies seemed like something we thought we could bear.

That night we kept talking in the darkness of our bedroom, Gerb asking hundreds of questions about the school: How was the food? How hard were the classes? What were the dorm rooms like? Was it easy to learn to march? I laughed and answered, trying to be as honest as I could while not scaring him away with the hard stuff that would be coming for him. I had decided that Valley Forge was good for me, and that I was lucky to be there. I was certain that it would be good for Gerb as well.

"But Reem," Gerb said just before we drifted off to sleep. "What about Mom? Do you think she'll be okay without me?"

I hesitated. I had been wondering the same thing. "You said she's in NA, right?" I said. "How long's it been?"

"Like, three months."

I raised my eyebrows. "That's a long time. Longer than she's been for ages."

"Yeah," said Gerb.

"And Washika's seven now. She's not a baby anymore."

"True," said Gerb.

I took a breath. "Listen, I know what it feels like. To think you have to stay. But like Lez always told us, if you get the chance to get out, you gotta take it. I think this is your chance, bro."

"I know," said Gerb. He was quiet for a moment. "I just worry."

"Me, too," I said. "I know."

———

It was coming up toward the end of summer, and I still didn't have my scholarship renewed. I knew that Lezlie was feverishly working on it, but Valley Forge was nearly forty thousand dollars a year. I started to think about other options. Maybe there was another school that had a polo program and might want me. Maybe I could stay on the farm and keep working for them. Maybe I would go home and actually try to make it through the local school so I could rejoin Work to Ride. The idea of returning back to the old neighborhood both repelled and intrigued me. There was definitely something appealing about going back to where I felt most at home, where I could be the version of myself that I was most familiar with. Also, I loved the Work to Ride barn, of course, and liked the idea of getting to see my family and Lez more often, but when I thought about being back in that school, or walking down those streets, the memory of night after night of panic and fear made me realize that I didn't want to return. I needed to find another way.

I hadn't told Gerb about this problem yet. I didn't want to worry him, or give him any reason to turn down Dennis's generous offer. I tried to shove the worry away. I told myself that Lezlie always came through when I needed her, that something would fall into place, but as each day ticked by and no one came forward to sponsor me, I suddenly realized it could very well just be Gerb at Valley Forge alone, and me back in The Bottom, starting all over again.

CHAPTER FIFTEEN

Wefound someone," Lezlie said to me over the phone. She sounded both thrilled and relieved. "A really accomplished alumnus, Stephen Bannerman. Assuming you keep up your grades, he's setting up a full scholarship for all your remaining time at Valley Forge."

When I heard this news, it felt exactly like when I was finally allowed to drop the fifty-pound rifle after a day of marching.

"What made him choose me?" I asked, excited. "Does he like polo?"

Lezlie paused. "Well . . . I wouldn't say he's a fan, exactly. But that's no big deal. No team to play on right now, anyway. What's important is that he is happy to sponsor you. In fact, he gave me a message to send you. He said to tell you, 'Don't let me down.'"

I blinked. "What's that supposed to mean?"

"It just means do your best! Just like you always do."

"Right," I said. "Okay."

"That's all anyone can ask of you, kiddo."

———

I returned to school, invited into Leadership Detail as I'd hoped I would be. I got Gerb through his plebe weeks the best I could. The school was smart enough to separate us so that I didn't have direct supervision over him, but I made sure everyone knew he was my brother. I also sought him out when I could, so he had someone to talk to. I snuck him my phone and let him call Lezlie and our mom. When my mom or Lezlie sent him a package, I saw that he got all his snacks. I used my rank for him in whatever way I could. His first six weeks weren't easy, but I let him know that he wasn't alone.

I'd like to say that I was kinder and gentler to all the plebes, but that would be a lie. The plebe system is meant to do certain things: tear you down so you can be built back up, cement your loyalty to your school and your classmates, teach you the basics of being a good and obedient soldier, and weed out the people who really should not be at the school. I came down on the plebes just like my squad leader had come down on me, because as a ranked cadet, it was my job to make sure the new kids toughened up. Still, sometimes I'd see a plebe who seemed like they were at the end of their rope, or had an expression on their face that told me they were about to either cry or puke or give up and go home, and I'd try to sneak them a kind word or a smile of commiseration. One thing I'd learned going through my own plebe experience was that just the smallest bit of encouragement could feel like a miracle when you're going through hell.

I had cracked the code and I was doing everything I was

supposed to do. My grades were the highest they'd ever been, I was playing soccer and lacrosse again, and I had friends from every social group at the school. People joked about how I was the bridge between the cliques. I could slide in between different groups with ease. I was fine with the shit bags, I was comfortable with the ranked cadets, the jocks, and the geniuses, and I could even talk with the staff like they were my peers. I had rank, and that left me with more time on my hands than I'd ever had at the school. I was allowed to go into town, to try to meet girls and get a decent meal every once in a while. Sometimes the other cadets I was with would try to talk me into returning to school late, or having a beer, or any number of things that I knew would get me into trouble, but I was never tempted. I was done being brought up before the board. I was determined never to do another tour. I was going to do everything right this year.

—

Francisco, my Robitussin-addicted roommate, had been expelled at the end of our first year when the school had finally caught on to his taste for cough syrup. Since then, I had been assigned three more roommates, all of whom seemed to have a weakness for drugs of various kinds and all of whom ended up being kicked out of the school.

Before each new assignment, my tac officer would call me into his office. He'd tell me about all the ways my new roommate was struggling and then tell me that he expected me to be a good influence, rub off on them in a positive kind of way.

This was something the school did, pairing up the troubled kids with cadets who seemed to have it more together. I understood that VF had its methods, that they counted on peer-to-peer influence to do a lot of the work for them, and I didn't mind, exactly. Despite their issues, all of these guys were nice enough, and I had grown up knowing plenty of addicts, so that didn't scare me much. I honestly don't know if I helped any of them while they lived with me, but at least I was never tempted to enable or partake. I had seen what drugs did to a person and had no interest in testing that out on myself.

It did sometimes make me feel uneasy, though. I'd watch my roommates when I knew they were high, seeing the same slack face and empty eyes that my mom and grandma used to get when they were using. It brought back some things I didn't really want to think about. It made me wonder how things were going back home.

—

My grandmother Sheila, my mom's mom, had always been a huge presence in my life. Grandma and my grandpa Jeffrey were off and on over the years, coming together and apart, but they both managed to be there for my mom and the rest of us in their own ways. Grandpa was around a bit, and he'd help out financially whenever he could, but Grandma and my mom were especially close. Even though my grandma was an addict like my mother (although unlike my mother, she didn't ever really try to get clean) she'd been taking care of us and providing backup for my mom for years.

My grandma had a house of her own just a few blocks from Viola Street. It was a drug house—even more run down than our place, and constantly filled with people up to no good—but she didn't actually spend much time there. Between us and all our cousins, she was almost always at one of her kids' houses, sleeping on the floor and helping take care of her grandchildren. She had the same attitude as my mother; she didn't believe in shielding us from anything—good, bad, or ugly. She couldn't afford a car, so if she decided she needed to score drugs, she'd dress us in any random way—socks for gloves, too-small shirt with too-big pants, a scarf wrapped around our heads instead of a hat—and we'd go out walking. Sometimes for blocks and blocks. And when we got to where we were going, she'd line us up on the sidewalk and tell us to stay put while she did what she had to do.

Still, even with her addiction, she knew how to survive and she made sure we were surviving, too. Maybe we looked funny, but those mismatched clothes kept us warm. She never let us go hungry; she could make a meal out of nothing when she needed to. And even if she was stoned or high, if we were in her care, she never let us out of her sight. She still managed our mom, too. My mom might have been a grown woman with six half-grown kids of her own, but I don't know if she would have made it through all those years if my grandma hadn't been there to hold her up. Mom always said that my grandmother was her best friend.

My mom had been doing good lately, clean for the longest she'd ever been, and even though I knew she worried about David and Bee and Kareema, and missed me and Gerb, she'd been pretty cheerful whenever she called us at school. She'd chat about this and that, tell us about something funny Washika had done, talk about her new job, and ask us questions about our classes.

"I was thinking about me and Washika making a move," she told me once. We'd been talking about how the neighborhood felt even more dangerous lately. How things had changed for the worse. "Go to the country. Get me a small house with a garden. I have a friend who lives in a little town in Jersey. Says it's real peaceful."

For a little while, I allowed myself to start thinking that she'd be okay. That maybe her sobriety would really stick. I let my guard down, relaxed a little. Decided that maybe things would turn out for once. But I should have known better. Things never seemed to turn out in The Bottom.

My grandma died of a brain aneurysm in the fall of that year, and then, not long after, my grandfather died of cancer. I was sad, of course. I loved them both, but I barely had time to grieve their loss because I was so worried about how my mom would take things.

She'd been in agony at their funerals, weeping over their coffins, wailing her heartbreak, even passing out at one point. All my siblings (who were not in jail) and cousins were there, but there was hardly room for anyone else to have feelings because my mom's were so intense.

———

"Reem? Reem? That you, baby?" It was late. She was slurring. I could tell she'd been drinking, and maybe more.

I kept my voice low so I wouldn't bother my roommate. "Yeah, it's me, Mom. How you been?"

"I miss them, Reem. I miss them so much." She started to cry.

I swallowed back my own tears. I never could hear my mom cry without responding in turn.

It became a ritual. That whole year, almost every night, I would hold the phone and listen to the soft sound of my mother's grief, the flatness of her depression, the stutter and slurring of her addiction. I was still a kid. I didn't know what to say to make it better. I didn't know how to change what was happening to her, so I just did the only thing I could. I stayed on the line and listened as long as she needed me.

CHAPTER SIXTEEN

I was informed that Stephen Bannerman, the man who had underwritten my education, wanted to meet with me. He and his wife asked that I join them and the president of our school at President McGeorge's house for dinner.

I dressed carefully that night, giving my uniform a fresh press and shining my shoes and belt buckle until I could see my own face in them. I was nervous. Lezlie hadn't told me much about Bannerman, except that he was a banker, and that he actually provided quite a few other kids at VF with scholarships. I wondered if he had dinner with all those kids, too.

As I sat at the dining-room table with the president, the president's wife, and Stephen Bannerman and his wife, I thought to myself that I was glad that VF had taught me exactly how a cadet should eat. I smiled inwardly, remembering how frustrated I'd been with those instructions when I'd first received them, but I was grateful that it wasn't like the

Hamptons, not knowing what fork to use or what to do with my hands.

I guessed that Stephen Bannerman was somewhere in his sixties, with steel-gray hair and faded blue eyes. His wife, Jeanette, was a blonde with a bright smile, wearing a yellow sweater. From the deferential way the president spoke to them both, I assumed that they had a great deal of influence at the school. They were very interested in me, peppering me with questions as I enjoyed the fact that I was getting a real meal for once instead of having to eat mess food.

They asked how school was going, what subjects I enjoyed. They said they heard my brother was also at the school and asked how he was adjusting.

"So, what are your plans for after Valley Forge?" asked Bannerman as I dug into a piece of chocolate cream pie for dessert. "What schools are you considering?"

"Cornell is my top pick, sir," I said. "I hope to play polo there."

Bannerman frowned. "Polo?"

I nodded. "Yes, sir. I played polo here until the program was cut this year."

Bannerman cleared his throat. "Yes, that was mentioned to me." He smiled. "Cornell is a fine school. It would be quite the accomplishment to be accepted."

"My coach at Work to Ride, Lezlie Hiner, said that I could potentially get a scholarship from Cornell based on my riding, sir."

He raised his eyebrows. "And you're still playing polo at this place—Work to Ride?"

"No, sir. I am not currently playing polo anywhere."

He nodded. "I see. Well, that's fine, really. Don't want to

end up a groom living up above someone's stable, do you?"
He laughed at his own joke, looking sideways at his wife un-
til she joined him. "What about military school, eh? West
Point? Annapolis?"

I shook my head. "I don't really see myself at a military
school, sir."

"But that's where you are now!" interjected his wife.

"Yes, ma'am, and while I am very grateful for my education here, I don't think that's in my plan for the future."

"It's a good way to learn discipline, Cadet."

"No offense, sir, but I believe that I have learned plenty of
discipline at Valley Forge."

He laughed. "Indeed, but I have seen that it can be forgotten once cadets leave."

"Did you, Stephen?" asked the president. "Forget the discipline you learned here?'

Bannerman shook his head. "No, but I made it a point to
exercise that discipline regularly in various ways. Not every
cadet is willing to do such a thing."

"Now, now, Stephen," said Jeanette. "Let's not put too
much pressure on poor Kareem."

"I just want to make sure I get my money's worth," Bannerman answered. He smiled at me and I felt a tiny twinge of
panic in my gut.

I swallowed. "I will do my best, sir."

He nodded. "I certainly hope so." He met my eyes. "Don't
let me down, Cadet."

—

I walked back toward my dorm feeling confused. I'd thought
the reason that Bannerman had agreed to provide my

scholarship was that he had been impressed with me, saw my potential. As far as I was concerned, there was nothing more impressive about me than what I could do on horseback, but he obviously didn't feel the same way. In fact, I couldn't tell if he had liked me at all.

It was a beautiful night out, dark and clear. There was no moon, so the stars seemed especially bright. I stopped for a moment to admire them, still thinking about Bannerman. Maybe he didn't like horses, I thought as I searched the sky. Some people didn't. Or maybe he just didn't know much about polo. That wouldn't be anything new, I reminded myself.

I blinked at the stars, thinking how I almost never noticed them when I was home. I saw the warm lights of the barn down the hill and decided to change course.

There were still some horses for the cavalry program in the stables at VF, and even though I didn't participate in it, I couldn't resist checking in on them from time to time. I'd been wandering over to the barn at all sorts of strange hours, peeking in whenever I could.

It was quiet when I got there. I knew the horses had already been put away for the night. But I slid the door open and stuck my head in anyway, taking deep, restorative breaths of that sweet barn smell. There was one bare lightbulb left burning, and I squinted through the shadows at the few lonely horses housed toward the back. I listened to the soft sounds as they shifted in their stalls, contentedly chewing their hay. I looked at all the empty places, the space where Cholo should have been, the ghostly spots that the polo ponies used to inhabit.

I stood in that doorway for a long time before I slid the door shut and turned back around.

I'd just have to make sure Bannerman understood how important horses were to me, I decided as I walked back up the hill. Once he realized how good I was really was, how much polo meant to me, he'd surely change his mind.

——

The days went by and everything was mostly fine. I still missed my grandparents and had to steel myself against the nightly calls from my mother, but the good things in my life were really good: Gerb had made it through the first six weeks and was settling in nicely, my grades were solid, I had friends. With my new rank, I was enjoying school in a way I never had before.

So when the panic attacks started again, I couldn't understand why.

The thing about panic and anxiety is that it's both mental and physical, and the physical part has a way of getting you in its grips before you even know what's going on. By the time I could tell myself it was all in my head, my body had already taken over. The fear coursing through me, sending chills up my back, making my hands and knees feel weak, my heart go wild, and my lungs refuse to work, felt like nothing so much as it felt like I was having a heart attack. Or at least, what I imagined a heart attack felt like. Over and over again, my body fooled my mind into thinking it was dying.

I thought that coming to Valley Forge had ended panic attacks for me. Despite all the difficulties at the school, I felt safe on this campus, safe in my dorm room. Things were scheduled and predictable and I could be sure of my days.

There is probably no good place to have a panic attack, but when I was younger, they were mostly contained to my own bed late at night. They were triggered by darkness; they were tied to Mecca's death. I might have carried the aftereffects of exhaustion and anxiety throughout my day, but at least I could count on being able to keep these fits of misery private.

I was walking across campus when the first one hit. I was late for a class, and hauling myself up the steep incline of Suicide Hill, the place where so many plebes had collapsed and given up. I don't know what triggered me, exactly, but suddenly I went from being slightly out of breath from the climb, to gasping for air, and so dizzy, I thought I would fall to my knees.

I knew what it was. I recognized it and ordered myself to calm the fuck down. I tried for deep breaths. I tried to think distracting thoughts. I tried all the little tricks I had taught myself over the years back in Philly. For a minute, I just doubled over, resting my head on my knees.

A cadet I knew walked past, laughing at me. "What the hell? Are you hungover, Rosser? Suicide Hill gonna make you puke?"

I glanced up and smiled weakly. "Yeah," I said. My voice was barely a croak. "Big night."

He laughed again. "You're a wild man!" he called over his shoulder as he trudged up the hill.

Having to talk to someone else knocked me back into reality. The adrenaline surge receded and the breath whooshed back into my lungs. I slowly straightened back up, and then just stood on the hill for a moment, taking deep breaths.

I thought about going to the health center, but then I imagined trying to explain what was going on. I thought about the doctor I'd seen when I was younger who had said it was all in my head. Valley Forge did not seem like a good place to announce that something was messing with my sanity.

—

It started happening more and more often. Sometimes at night, after reveille. Sometimes during the day, during class, or drills, or practice. I got good at hiding what was going on, inwardly feeling like shit, but quietly pushing through the cold fear in full view of everyone. If it got really bad, I would claim an upset stomach and stay in a bathroom until I could breathe again.

Only Gerb noticed, squinting at me one day in the mess hall while I sat, ignoring my lunch, clenching my hands, feeling the sweat pop out on my forehead, silently counting backward in my head.

"You sick?" he asked. "Did you eat something bad?"

I shook my head, not trusting myself to speak.

He squinted at me. "Yo, Reem. What's wrong?"

"I gotta go," I muttered, lurching up and leaving my tray on the table.

Gerb was right behind me. "Reem!" he called as I hurried ahead of him. "Kareem!"

I stopped, slumping against the hallway wall. I closed my eyes. I could hear Gerb catch up with me.

"What the hell, bro?"

"I just don't feel right," I whispered.

I opened my eyes and looked at Gerb. He stared at me for a moment.

"Maybe you should go see Lezlie," he finally said.

The barn. Just picturing it, I felt my shoulders slump in relief. "Yeah, that's a good idea," I agreed.

—

I asked for a weekend pass and took a bus back to the city. I remember the ride down, staring out the window as we passed a long, stubbly cornfield. I remember imagining I was outside, looking in, riding Cholo, galloping along and keeping pace with the bus. I could feel it, smell it, hear it: me and my pony, running the field.

—

I hadn't told Lezlie I was coming. It was late in the day and the barn was mostly empty, but I saw the glow of light from her office. I walked to the back of the barn.

"Lez."

She looked up, blinking in surprise. It felt good to see my coach and mentor—my other mother, as we always called her. Her hair was starting to be more gray than blond. "Kareem! What in the world?" She popped up from behind her desk and hurried over to hug me.

I hugged her back, trying not to feel like the little kid who used to hang off her all the time. "I got a weekend pass. Just thought I'd come for a visit."

She stepped back and looked up at me. Her eyebrows knitted together. Her sharp gaze missed nothing. Suddenly she tipped her head and winked. "You want to meet the horses?"

We laughed as we walked back toward the stalls. This wasn't a barn like the one in Connecticut. It was messier, rougher; everywhere I looked something needed fixing or mending or cleaning, but I didn't care. I could breathe here.

It was home to me. We walked from stall to stall, rubbing the horses' noses and scratching necks. I stopped to pat Buck.

"He got a new kid to torture?" I asked as he fondly nuzzled at my hair.

She laughed. "Of course. He'll be throwing off kids until he dies."

"Where's Cholo?" I asked, looking around for my pony. I'd shipped him back to the barn before I left for Connecticut the summer before.

Lezlie smiled. "Come see," she said, pointing out the door.

We walked outside and I stepped up onto the fence and looked into the ring where Bee and David had taught me to ride.

There was a young girl out there alone, practicing on my horse, tripping round and round in the mud, her long braids sticking out from under her helmet and spilling down her back. Cholo was patiently trotting along, teaching her to ride. They reminded me of the way I used to ride Angel, determined not to do more than move like a turtle around the ring.

Lezlie looked at me, grinning. "Who would have thought he'd settle down enough to teach beginners, right?" She cupped her mouth with her hands. "Nice, Kiara!" she yelled. "Try to stay a little more centered in the saddle, and don't cut your corners!"

The girl didn't even look up. She just nodded and kept riding, the pink tip of her tongue poking out of the corner of her mouth in concentration.

We silently walked the rest of the grounds. With every step, I could feel the tension I had been carrying dissipate. My muscles were looser; every breath I took felt cleaner and deeper. The sun was low and the light was thin, a pale gold mixed with purple shadow. I could smell the manure and the feed and the fine silt of dried mud that encased everything this time of year. I could hear the way the big trees around the barn squeaked and rubbed against each other in the frigid late-autumn breeze. I looked over at the soccer field across the street. I could tell kids had been riding in it. It was churned to mud.

"How's the team doing?" I asked Lezlie.

She laughed and shrugged. "We're still trying," was all she said.

We went back into the barn. I looked up into the hayloft for a moment, my eyes resting on the rafters. Lezlie's gaze followed mine.

"You can go on up, if you like," she said lightly. "I've got some work to finish in the office."

I climbed up to the top of the stairs and stopped, unable to go over the threshold. After Mecca died, I had done my best to avoid coming up here. It had seemed too painful, seeing the places where we had spent our happiest hours.

I hung back for a moment, probing my feelings, realizing that they weren't quite so unbearably sharp anymore. I saw a small black barn cat curled up on a bale of hay, one who had been fat and sleek when I'd first met him, many years before, but now was half his original size, an aged pile of rough, haphazardly cleaned fur and jutting bones.

Without thinking about it, I walked over and sat down next to him on the bale of hay. "Yo, Darth Vader," I said as the cat happily crept into my lap. I petted him, smoothing down his feathery coat, and he emitted a rusty purr.

That cat and I sat there a long time, letting the barn go

dark around us, listening to the quiet movement of the horses in their stalls. I watched the little girl who had been riding Cholo lead him back in, brush him out, and put him into his stall for the night before cheerfully saying goodbye to Lezlie and running out the door.

I gently picked Vader up and deposited him on the hay bale, and then climbed back down and walked over to my horse. Cholo's ears pricked as I approached and when I got closer, he neighed, his big trumpeting welcome sound.

"Hi, boy," I said as I leaned over the gate and kissed his velvety nose. Lezlie walked out of her office, checking each stall to make sure that everyone had hay and water.

Finally she walked over to where I was standing.

I dropped my hand, but Cholo reached out and nuzzled me with his soft nose. "Do you remember when my mom thought I had asthma?" I said to Lezlie.

She raised her eyebrows. "I remember that being discussed at some point. But didn't the tests come back negative?"

I nodded. "Yeah. I guess it was all in my head," I said. "That's what the doctor said. But I still couldn't breathe."

She waited.

I leaned my forehead against Cholo's neck for a moment. "I feel like that now. At school. It's real bad, Lez."

She was quiet for a moment and then said, "It's because you're not riding, kiddo."

I swallowed hard. "I know.

CHAPTER SEVENTEEN

Say that again, man! Come here and say it to my face!" Drea whipped around to glare at the six-foot-five white dude who had just passed us on the way to the arena.

I grabbed Drea's arm. "Yo, what are you doing?"

The big guy turned around. "I said your shoelace is untied."

Drea yanked his arm away from me and stepped back toward the giant, puffing his chest out. "Oh, so it's like that, eh? You really want to do this, then? Let's go!"

The giant squinted, looking totally bewildered.

I grabbed Drea harder this time, and Gerb took his other arm. We pulled him along the path.

"Bro, you have to stop doing that," I hissed.

"He was disrespecting me!"

"Your shoelace *is* untied!" Gerb pointed out.

"And that is nobody's business! Maybe I happen to want

it to be untied!" He pulled his arm out from our grasp as we kept walking. "I coulda taken him," he muttered.

I looked at my six-foot-tall, muscle-bound teammate. "Yeah, you could have. And then we would have been thrown out of the tournament."

He shrugged. "Don't want to play anyway."

I threw my hands up in frustration. "We got a chance today, man."

He looked at me, a teasing smile breaking across his face. He imitated my voice, making it way higher than it actually was. "'*We got a chance!*' Oh, do we, Reem? Do we have a chance?"

I shrugged, defensive. "Well, we might."

He laughed, playfully bumping my shoulder with his own. "Keep dreaming, bro."

——

Lezlie had come through for me again. After my visit to the barn, she had called President McGeorge and arranged for a dispensation. Gerb and I were to be allowed to go home every weekend and play on the new Work to Ride polo team she had formed: Gerb, one of Gerb's best friends Drea, and me as team captain.

When I first told Gerb, he almost looked like he was going to cry. "We get to go home? We get to ride?"

I'm not going to lie, I felt a little choked up myself. Apparently my little brother had been missing the game as much as I had.

The first time we walked back into the barn, I half expected a party with noisemakers and balloons to greet us, it felt so monumental in my head, but it was just a quiet Saturday morning, same as usual.

Lezlie was out in the ring, giving a lesson. The barn kids were doing their morning chores, shoveling shit and hauling buckets of water, grooming their ponies. Gerb saw some friends he knew and walked over to greet them.

I took a quick moment. Closed my eyes, allowed myself to breathe in that sweet air and feel the warmth of the ponies radiating around me. Then I opened my eyes, picked up a pitchfork, and walked over to Cholo in his stall. Because home wasn't the place where they threw you a party every time you returned. Home was the place where you could slip right back into normal.

Cholo was munching some hay, but he looked up at me and nickered softly.

"How about it, boy?" I said as I reached in and scratched his neck. "You ready to ride?"

—

It was exactly what I needed. I had to work harder than ever to keep up with my classes because I was playing all weekend, but I didn't care. My panic attacks almost immediately stopped, and from the time Gerb and I first walked back into that barn, I felt like myself again.

I had grand visions for this team. Thinking back on my time playing with Bee, I kept dwelling on that last game at Cornell with Bee and Andy, how close we had come to winning the championship. I knew that I wasn't as good as Bee had been, but after two years of playing at VF and my time in Connecticut, I thought I was almost there. Gerb was still small and a little clumsy, but he was a strong player, too; he had Bee's fearlessness on horseback.

Drea Taylor, however, was a problem. I'd known Drea since he was a little kid—he was one of Gerb's best friends—and he'd always been something of a problem. His mom was an addict, and his dad wasn't in the picture. Drea had it tough from the beginning, basically forced to raise himself up. From the time they were little, he and Gerb and another kid from our block, Brandon Rease, were inseparable. They ran around the neighborhood in a trio. Brandon's mom, Tanya, who was much more involved with her son than either my mom was with Gerb or Drea's mom was with him, tried to play the de facto parent for all three of them, luring them in at night and doing her best to keep them out of trouble, but there were plenty of times when Gerb and Drea got tired of being cooped up and snuck out on their own to raise hell.

I've never met a guy who liked to fight more than Drea. He regularly showed up at the barn with black eyes and skinned knuckles. Drea attended a school for children with behavioral problems, so he had plenty of chances to get into it there, but even if we were just walking down the block together, he'd meet every eye and step into anyone's path. Considering where we lived, this was, of course, dangerous in a way that stretched far beyond the possibility of a split lip or a broken rib, but Drea didn't care. It seemed he was full of some bitter emotion that only felt relieved when he was either hitting or being hit.

It's funny, because I actually understood Drea. Despite the obvious differences in our demeanors, I knew what it was like to be filled with something that you couldn't control. I knew what it felt like to keep pushing that feeling down, ignoring it and pretending it wasn't there, until it got so bad that it boiled up into something scalding and painful. The way that happened to me was different than the way it happened to Drea; my reaction was inward and solitary, whereas his was aimed outward at anyone who had the misfortune to get in his way. But like recognized like; I understood that when Drea was fighting, it wasn't because he was a bad or violent person, it was because he was desperate to shake the dread and anxiety that lived curled up in his belly day in and day out.

Horses and polo were the bulwark against my own fears. It had become very clear to me that I couldn't do without them. Something about both controlling and connecting with an animal made me feel brave. Riding washed my anxiety away. Having to attune to something literally bigger than myself allowed me to keep things in context.

I think the horses helped Drea, too. Certainly, he had committed to the barn in a way that he had never committed to anything else before. He had talent, as well. He was strong and swift, and had great reflexes. He was a natural athlete. He had almost everything he needed to become a great player.

That was why it was so bizarre to watch him get into a game and completely shut down. This big, buff dude who was afraid of nothing on the ground transformed into a giant baby on a pony. He refused to take any chances. He wasn't willing to hook another player's stick or even consider attempting a rideoff, and he was so worried someone would come after him and knock him around that he basically gave the ball away. I was convinced that if he could have stood in a corner and just watched us play from horseback and called it a game, that would have suited him just fine.

Of course, Gerb and I had our own issues on the field. Gerb had that ridiculous temper that flared whenever we started to lose (and that first year, we lost all the fucking time). I can't count the number of fouls he got for bad language and arguing with the umps. Lezlie had to pull that kid out almost every other game.

My problem was that I had no idea how to captain a team. I thought the captain's job was to be Superman—everywhere at once, playing every position, making every goal, blocking every member of the other team. Bee had been the only captain I'd ever really respected, and that was the way he had played. But what I didn't get was that Bee played that way because he could. He was one of those rare people who could singlehandedly win a game. He earned the name Killer Bee because he was lightning fast and stung like hell; he barely needed his teammates and he wasn't going to bother to pretend he did. So I thought this was the way to captain. Even when I'd had other captains at VF, I was so sure that I was a better player than them that I still tried to run the field. I was completely convinced that no game was going to be won if I wasn't the rider out there winning it.

It was no wonder our team sucked, and it was no wonder that when we played, we were seen as a novelty act. I hated the way people treated us back then. We were suffering the tyranny of low expectations and it seemed we could do nothing to prove those expectations wrong. Past teams from Work to Ride had encountered blatant, ugly racism, over which Lezlie had raised a huge stink. By the time our team came along, the prejudice was quieter, and more insidious. We were simply never treated as real horsemen. I couldn't shake the feeling that everyone was just waiting for us to give up and go back to the street corner they imagined we had come from. Maybe because so many of us did.

—

"Drea! DREA! Hook the mallet! It's practically going to land in your lap!"

I watched Drea look up at the rapidly approaching ball and then back up his horse and let it fall right in front of him, where it was almost immediately whooshed up by an opposing team player. Drea didn't even raise his mallet.

"Come on, Drea!" I burst out.

Gerb's exclamation from across the field was louder.

"DREA! Would you stop being such a pussy-ass pussy and get your head in the game?"

Whistles. Fouls. Lezlie forced to practically drag Gerb off the field. Another two-on-three game that we lost by embarrassing numbers.

—

It was a terrible season. We played all up and down the coast, piling into Lezlie's car and going from game to game each weekend.

We lost almost every single game.

We each had our strong points as players (even Drea could play when he got up the nerve), but we just couldn't seem to come together as a team.

Lezlie did her best to coach us through, but our issues seemed beyond her repair. I wondered if she regretted creating the team. She had pushed back some other Work to Ride members to give us our shot and we were royally screwing it up.

I knew that Lezlie truly believed that someday she would put together a team that would bring home the championship trophy to the barn. She dreamed of it, and I really wanted to do that for her—I imagined it practically every time we made a goal—but I was pretty sure that particular fantasy would not be coming true that year.

—

"I'm worried about Drea," whispered Gerb.

We were sitting together in the library at VF, supposedly doing homework. Gerb was suffering through the same academic issues I'd had as an eighth grader—he'd started out years behind—so I was helping him with his math.

"Of course you're worried about Drea," I said back, pulling his workbook toward me so I could judge just how truly he didn't understand negative numbers. "He fights anything he sees and he's the reason we lose every game."

Gerb half smiled. "You know he's not the only reason."

I rolled my eyes. "Okay, he's *most* of the reason."

"Bro, I am worried about Drea because he told me his mom is real bad lately. I don't even know if he's getting anything to eat."

I frowned. Lezlie had once told me that the hardest part of running Work to Ride wasn't what happened at the barn; it was what happened when everyone went home. Temptation and danger were everywhere and there wasn't anything Lezlie, or I, could do about it.

"I think he might start dealing," said Gerb.

"Well, he makes his—"

"—own choices," interrupted Gerb. "Yeah, I know what

Coach Lezlie would say, bro. What I'm more interested in is what you, as our team captain, might think about it."

I frowned. "Lez won't let him go hungry."

Gerb waved his hand like he was shooing away a mosquito. "Sure, if Drea actually told her he was hungry she would take care of things. But you know he ain't ever gonna do that."

"So why don't you tell her?"

Gerb shook his head. "Come on. You think Drea would be down with that?"

"So what do you want me to do? Make him a sandwich?"

"Don't be an asshole," shot back Gerb. "I want you to talk to him. Figure out a way to keep him at the barn."

I laughed. "You playin'? When have I ever been able to keep anyone at the barn?"

"You the captain now," said Gerb. I could tell he was getting frustrated. "This isn't the same as Bee or David or Kareema. You in charge now."

"I am not," I said. "I mean, sure, on the field, I guess, but not anywhere else. And besides, Drea hardly even listens to me on the field. I don't know what you think I could say that would keep him off the street corner if that's what he decides he wants to do."

"You make it sound like he has a choice," grumbled Gerb.

"Everyone has a choice," I shot back.

Gerb glared at me and clenched his jaw. I could see the little muscle fluttering in his cheek. "Including you," he said. "You have a choice to try to help Drea."

"I'm the captain of his polo team, not his therapist."

"Drea doesn't have—"

"I *know,* Gerb," I spluttered. "Just tell him to go visit Mom. She'll make him a plate."

"Jesus," said Gerb. "What is wrong with you? Why can't you see the point?"

"I do see the point," I said. "I just don't know what you think I can do about it! Lezlie sent Bee all the way to Texas. She had David literally move in with her. They both still did what they wanted to do. Nothing works when someone makes up their mind to leave, okay? The only thing I've seen that keeps anyone safe is fucking military school, and I'm pretty sure we're not going to get Drea into Valley Forge!"

Gerb stared at me for a moment and then looked away, quickly brushing at his eyes. "I know," he finally said. His voice was low. "You're right."

"I wish I wasn't." My voice was softer now. "I wish I had any idea how to make someone stay safe. Drea is like a brother. I don't want him to go, either."

Gerb sighed. "Maybe he'll pull it together and stay."

I nodded. "Maybe. You never know."

After a moment I pushed the workbook back toward him, tapping the page with my index finger. "Do this problem again. You got it wrong."

CHAPTER EIGHTEEN

D rea didn't stay. It went down just as we knew it would. First he started skipping school, then he started showing up late at the barn, then he started missing whole days, and then, he was gone. Some things you could see coming from a mile away and they still managed to break your heart.

Gerb took it hard. Polo season was over. We weren't playing any more games, but we still went back to the barn to practice on weekends. For a long time, he seemed diminished; he was quiet and distant. He wasn't the rider I knew. I didn't get after him about it. I knew what this particular kind of loss felt like, and I knew there wasn't much to do but wait it out and hope that both Gerb and Drea would be okay in the end.

—

"Look at this." Gerb pulled out a package from his post office box. "Dennis sent me something."

"You do not know how lucky you are to have him as your sponsor," I said as I watched Gerb open the brand-new pair of riding gloves and try them on. "Bannerman made me do another lunch with him and spent the whole time talking about whether I should join the Army or the Marines. Then instead of saying goodbye he said, 'Don't let me down.' Just like last time. I am pretty sure the dude thinks it's his catchphrase."

"Did you tell him you're riding again?" said Gerb as he flexed his hands and admired his gloves.

I shook my head. "No way. I'm keeping my grades up like I promised. I'm not letting him down. He don't need to track what I'm doing on the weekends. Oh, and by the way, he also made a point of telling me that if I slip below a B minus average, he'll yank my scholarship."

Gerb's eyes bugged a little. "A B minus? I'd be psyched if I managed to get that this term. You right. I'm lucky to have Dennis. He said as long as I'm trying as hard as I can, he doesn't care what my GPA is."

I snorted. "You got it easy, bro." I held out my hand. "Let me see those gloves."

——

Back when Brandon Rease finally convinced his mom to let him join Work to Ride, Gerb and I put him through a hazing process that made me think we'd learned a little too much from Valley Forge.

"First you need Lezlie to give you papers to fill out," I told him. "But you can't just ask for them. You have to be recommended by at least two current members at the barn."

Brandon blinked. "Just for the application papers?"

Gerb nodded, a serious look on his face. "It's very important that you don't try to get around this process by asking Lezlie directly, because if you do, you'll just have to get three recommendations instead of one."

He was pulling all of this out of his ass, of course, but Brandon didn't know that. He bought everything we were telling him.

"Well, at least I know you and Reem and Drea," he said. "That's three."

I jumped in. "No, sorry, you can't have two recommendations from the same family."

Gerb hid a smile and looked like he wanted to give me a high five for my contribution.

Brandon frowned. "Well, how am I supposed to do that? I need two, but I only know the three of you."

"Well," said Gerb. "You could ask Drea, plus one of us, plus Kareema. Lezlie counts the girls as separate from the family."

"What?" said Brandon. "Why?"

I was doing my best not to bust out laughing.

"Never mind that," said Gerb hurriedly. He could see me starting to crack up and didn't want to give it away. "What you need now is to figure out how you're going to convince us to give you those recommendations so you can get the papers."

Brandon looked puzzled. "I mean, aren't you just going to do it?"

I cocked my head. "Well, I dunno," I said. "We might need some proof that you're serious about the barn. We're not interested in anyone who isn't super dedicated."

"Yo, you know how serious I am about riding. I snuck out behind my mom's back just two days ago so I could watch you guys play."

"That's true," said Gerb. "And that was very brave of you, goin' against your mama. We all know what a hard-ass Tanya can be."

I laughed.

"Watch it," growled Brandon.

"Okay, okay," I said. "I have an idea. A way you can show us how tough you are." I pointed across the street at a small vegetable garden behind a sagging wire fence. "You see those peppers? I asked Mr. Jackson about them the other day and he said they ghost peppers. Like, the hottest hot peppers in the world."

Brandon frowned. "And?"

"And," I said, "If you can eat one—"

"Two!" said Gerb quickly. "One for every recommendation."

"Right," I nodded. "If you eat two—"

"Without spitting them out or puking them back up," added Gerb.

"Yes," I nodded solemnly. "They have to stay in your stomach until they come out the other end."

"Which will also hurt like hell, I've heard," said Gerb.

"You do that, and we'll go straight to the barn and tell Lezlie to give you the application," I finished.

Brandon lifted an eyebrow. "What about Reema's part of the recommendation?"

"Oh, she'll do it later. After we tell her what you did to earn it," said Gerb, waving his hand in the air like it was no big deal.

"Yeah, no problem," I said.

Brandon looked at us suspiciously. "Fine. But someone else has to go steal the peppers. I don't want to get chased by Mr. Jackson. He run fast for an old guy."

"No problem!" Gerb said cheerfully. He ran across the street, lifted the bottom of the wire fence, and was back with the peppers in no time. "Here," he said as he presented the small, gleaming red fruits to Brandon. "All yours, bro."

Brandon took them in his hand and stared at them for a second, and then, in one quick move, he threw them both into his mouth, chomped maybe four times, and swallowed.

"Dude!" shouted Gerb.

"Whoa! Both at once!" I said.

Brandon's eyes welled up with tears that immediately spilled over.

"Oh my God," he gasped. He opened his mouth, fanning desperately with both hands. "Fuck!" he croaked. "Fuck!"

We burst out laughing as he grabbed his tongue with his hand and looked like he was trying to pull it out of his head. He started to gag, his shoulders convulsing with every retch and burp. "Jesus fucking Christ!" he howled.

"Keep them down, Brandon!" yelled Gerb.

"You can do it, bro!" I cheered. "You got this, man!"

Brandon bent over, his head practically resting on his knees. "I need . . . I need . . ." He swallowed convulsively and then looked up at us, his eyes swimming in tears. "Milk," he gasped. "Home. See . . . later . . . barn." And he took off running, accompanied by the sound of our whoops of laughter chasing after him.

—

Unlike the rest of us, Brandon was a straight-A student, a kid who almost never got into trouble, who listened to his mom (who, despite our teasing, was someone we all loved and respected) and pretty much always did the right thing. He wanted to ride with us more than anything, but Tanya wasn't so sure she trusted Lezlie or the idea that her son would be okay out of her sight at the barn. She loved me and Gerb, but she thought we were trouble and she knew that we always tried to pull Brandon right along with us. So it took her a minute before Brandon wore her down and she finally let him sign up. By the time he started learning to ride, he was a couple years behind me and Gerb and had some serious catching up to do.

That all said, when Lez told us at the beginning of my junior year that she was moving up Brandon to take Drea's place, I was thrilled. Drea had been riding longer, but I knew that Brandon was going to be the better player. He'd been playing catch-up with me and Gerb since he joined the barn, and he worked his ass off doing it. He was always down to ride. On the days that the rest of us were grumbling about how it was too hot or too cold to get on a horse, Brandon was already out there in the ring doing the work. He wasn't precious about which horse he was assigned, either. Lezlie could give him anyone, good, bad, or ugly, and he'd get right on without complaining. When he got thrown off—which was often and sometimes violently in the beginning—he'd pop right up and insist on climbing back into that saddle and just keep going on. His work ethic was undeniable and his heart and determination to learn were unmatched.

—

"REACH FOR IT, BRANDON! Don't just let Kareem take it! Gerb, you get in there and ride defense!"

It was one of our first practices together as a new team. We were out on the soccer field across from the barn. It was still early fall, but the forecast said snow in the next couple of days and it looked like we'd face our annual problem—no indoor space to practice once the ice and snow hit—even earlier this year.

"Kareem, you should have been able to block that one!"

Lezlie was standing in her usual place, off to the side, coaching us from across the field as we scrimmaged.

It was a cold and gray day. The sky was drizzling, not enough to call off practice, but just enough to make things low-key miserable as we rode. The grass was dead and brown beneath us and the autumn leaves looked matted and rusty in the dull light. Even Cholo felt slow and resentful on the field, like he'd rather be tucked up in his warm stall.

Brandon took the ball, and Gerb and I rode sluggishly side by side for a moment, following in his wake.

"Pick it up, guys!"

Brandon pulled back his mallet and then missed the ball altogether. I heard some hoots and mocking laughter. A few of the smaller kids had wandered over from the barn to stand in the rain and watch us play.

"Brandon! Focus! You missed it because you weren't paying enough attention!"

Shaking my head, I picked up the ball and started down the field, Gerb coming at me from one side and Brandon from the other. Gerb reached out and tried to hook my mallet.

"Crossed the line, Gerb!"

Gerb turned and glared at Lezlie. "I did not!"

I ignored my brother's tantrum and rode on.

It's just more of the same.

I thought things were going to be different with Brandon on the team, but we were still playing like shit.

I tried to get Cholo to go a little faster, but he stubbornly pretended he had no idea what I wanted from him and kept to a polite trot, dropping his head whenever I signaled he should pick up the pace. I dug my heels in a little harder and finally got him into a canter, but when I reached down to hit the ball again, he dropped his head and came to an abrupt halt, and I went sailing out through the air and right onto my ass.

"Kareem! You all right?"

I nodded and raised my hand to let Lezlie know I was fine. I could hear all the little kids laughing hysterically. They always loved it when one of the older players got dumped.

Gerb rode up to me, his tantrum forgotten. He had a huge grin on his face. The first I'd seen all day. "You riding Cholo or Buck?" he asked. "Can't tell."

Brandon joined us, trying hard to keep a straight face. "You okay, Reem?"

I stood up, my ass covered in mud. I looked over at Cholo, who was just standing there, cool as could be. He met my eyes, all innocence.

I took a deep breath as a I grabbed his reins. "Okay," I said to my teammates. "Let's try something different." I swung up onto Cholo's back and thought for a moment. "Let's . . . just pass the ball."

——

"YES! Fantastic, Gerb! Go!"

Gerb streaked down the field, galloping wildly but keeping the ball exactly where he wanted it.

"Good, bro! Now pass it on to Brandon!" I yelled.

He hit it over to Brandon, who was circling toward him

in a wide curve. Brandon picked it right up and started heading for the goal.

"Excellent, Brandon!" yelled Lezlie.

I came around the other side, left of the goal. "Okay, Brandon, now send it to me!"

He hit it nice and square and it came whistling over. I scooped it up and kept toward the goal. I was at an awkward angle, but I was feeling lucky, so I took the shot anyway. The ball looked like a small, white bird as it sailed through the goal posts. The kids cheered. For real this time.

Gerb rode around and picked the ball right back up and then passed it over to Brandon in one smooth hit. Brandon passed it back to me and I grinned as I picked it up and then sent it back to Gerb.

Back and forth, over and over, we sent that ball flying over the field, dancing between the three of us and our ponies, passing it from player to player like we were all of one mind. Me, Gerb, Brandon. Brandon, me, Gerb. Gerb, Brandon, me. We couldn't miss.

I'd never felt this kind of connection. I'd never ridden with a team like this. I laughed out loud, it felt so good.

Finally, Gerb hit the ball through the goal posts and Lezlie's whistle signaled an end to the chukker.

I took Cholo around the field at a trot and then a walk, cooling him down. As I passed Lezlie, I brought my horse to a halt and smiled down at her. I was covered with mud, and wet to the bone, but I didn't care.

"Got pretty quiet there at the end, Lez," I teased.

She shrugged, and with a little start of recognition, I saw that her eyes were bright with happy tears. "You guys had it," she said as she smiled at me. "All I needed to do was sit back and watch."

—

Our connection wasn't just on the practice field. We started to win, and I knew the new team was really going to fly when we started getting calls to play college teams instead of high schools. It was only early November, but we'd already been dominating the high-school circuit. So much so that word had gotten out and we were getting invites to scrimmage up and down the East Coast. I was surprised at first. I didn't understand why a college-level team full of two-and three-goal players would want to mess with us, but then I figured the coaches probably just wanted to use us to give their teams a confidence boost. We were good enough to give them a little competition, but we were still kids, so we were guaranteed to lose in the end.

That's what we believed, too, until we drove up to the University of Connecticut to scrimmage with their team. The team was tight and expected to place high in the intercollegiate championship that year. They looked sort of surprised when they met us, but were good natured enough about playing a bunch of kids. I could tell that they'd be the kind of team that allowed us a gentleman's goal now and then. I hoped our loss wouldn't be too ugly.

We rode out into the ring and the ump threw in the ball and just like that, I had it. I had it, and was speeding down the field, and I threw back my mallet and hit that ball as hard as I could, and all of a sudden, we had our first goal.

The crowd cheered and Gerb and Brandon yelled, and the opposing team looked shocked, but I figured I'd taken them by surprise. Surely they were gonna try little harder now that they'd seen we weren't totally green.

And they did. They tried harder and made some goals, too. But we still kept scoring. Brandon made a goal and Gerb made two goals and I hooked the ball away from their captain and danced it down the field and made another goal, myself. We got through three chukkers and they were only a point ahead.

That's when I got boarded. Slammed up against the wall by a pissed-off college senior who didn't like the fact that he was losing to a bunch of children. My shoulder was hurt and I was a little shaken up, but it was one of the best moments I ever had playing the game. We were playing well enough to send a four-goal player after my neck. It was only made better by the fact that I followed up that foul with the only two-point goal that I ever made.

We won that day. We won and our team walked away knowing that something pretty fucking magical was happening on the field. The three of us were playing the kind of polo we didn't know we were capable of. We realized that maybe we had a chance to go all the way.

—

With every win, people started treating us a little differently. They couldn't call us a novelty act or put our wins down as luck when we were undeniably and consistently taking the games. Despite our hand-me-down uniforms and messed-up gear, I started to feel really good about our team when we walked into a polo club together, ready to play. All those marches and drills had paid off, and I finally looked more like a young man and less like a scrawny kid. Gerb had hit his growth spurt and it seemed like he might actually end up taller than me. Brandon might have been a mama's boy underneath it all, but that didn't show when we rolled into the games, Brandon doing his best to imitate my and Gerb's military-school swagger and the stone-cold, don't-fuck-with-us expressions we'd mastered during plebe season. We finally felt like we were getting somewhere and people were giving us the credit we deserved.

With Brandon on board, I was doing a little better as a captain. It was easier for me to trust my teammates when they were performing so well on the field. And Gerb's temper, which had been such a problem when we were being stomped, practically disappeared now that we were winning. He might have been a sore loser but he was also an extremely gracious winner. You'd never know that he was a foul-mouthed meltdown machine from the way he was all smiles and handshakes and "Good game" at those closing ceremonies.

Let a game go well from the beginning, let us take the lead and hold it, let us keep our score high and the other team at bay the whole way through, and we would just keep winning against even the best teams we played. Shots came easy, the ponies sensed what we wanted before we even pulled the reins, and we ran those games like we'd choreographed the whole thing ahead of time. Not a step was out of place.

Even the occasional scrimmage where we could tell we were outmatched from the beginning wasn't so bad. We'd fall into line and grimly do what we could to make sure it wasn't a total shutout. It was less joyful, but we never got humiliated on the field like we used to be. Even Gerb could handle those kinds of losses.

It was actually the close games that killed us. It was the kind of game where the other team was matching us shot for shot, where we met players who mirrored our skills so that there was no way of predicting who would take the win. We still fell apart in those moments. We might do okay in the beginning, but by that last chukker, we would revert back to our worst habits and choke like we were all Brandon eating those peppers. The closer we were to winning, the more likely it was that we'd start making stupid mistakes. I'd lose focus and start running all over the field, trying to get in every shot and take on every player. Gerb would start muttering under his breath and swinging his mallet at nothing, getting ready to curse out whoever pissed him off the most, and Brandon, who was the consummate supporting player, wouldn't be able to do a thing because we were giving him absolutely nothing to work with. We wanted those games too much. It was the pressure of almost tasting the win that got to us. When it really mattered, we couldn't close.

It didn't help that once the ground froze and the snow fell, we also couldn't practice. The teams that we played against could get on their horses every day if they wanted and use their indoor rings to work out their kinks and issues. They had pro-level polo ponies to run their plays on and try out new shots. From November to April, which was pretty much the entirety of the polo season, we had to wait until we were actually playing a game on another team's horses to do any riding. Everything in between was just talk. We'd spend our weekend either winning or losing and then Gerb and I would return to Valley Forge and Lezlie would go back to the barn and Brandon would go back to Viola Street and we'd have to wait another week and go to a different club, and ride a new string of ponies, before we could try to correct anything we'd done wrong.

Still, even with all that, we were winning way more than we were losing and we easily progressed to the national championships. I was certain it would be our year.

———

We won our first-round game.

It was one of those games that felt like pinball; we just pinged from goal to goal. We were machines. We took the lead from the minute we hit the field and never gave it up. It honestly probably wasn't even that fun to watch, because there was never a question about who was going to win.

This was the farthest I'd ever been. This was a game ahead of what I'd won with Bee when we made it into the national championship. I could taste the win. I was absolutely certain we had what we needed to take that trophy back to Philly with us.

We were playing the Baltimore Polo Club next. They were the number-one-seeded team and we knew they were good, but coming off the last game we'd played, our confidence was sky high.

We rode out into the arena already sure we had it, loose and relaxed. The three of us were shooting each other grins and feeling buzzed. The opposing team seemed nervous. The team captain didn't meet my gaze when I faced him for the throw-in. I imagined he'd heard about our last game and was just hoping we wouldn't wipe the floor with his team.

Baltimore got the ball first and surprised us with a quick and easy score. The crowd roared and stomped and that shook me a little. I met Gerb and Brandon's eyes each in turn and nodded. *No time to fool around,* I communicated. *We need to get the lead and keep it.*

And we did. We scored two goals in a row and ended that chukker feeling good. We handed off our horses to be hot-walked and swung up onto our fresh ponies and headed right back out. But Baltimore wasn't going to make it easy. They were skilled and unpredictable players. Usually I could take the measure of a team pretty fast; I'd notice their weak points and try to ride in a way that showed Gerb and Brandon what I'd figured out so they could exploit them, too. But Baltimore didn't play that way. They never showed their asses. They were just loping along, easy as you please, matching us goal for goal.

By the third chukker, I knew we were in trouble. We were one point ahead, but we'd been trading the lead back and forth the whole way through. I told myself that we couldn't let the pressure get to us. I promised myself that I would pull it together and make sure we all played right. I could see Gerb violently swinging his mallet around from the corner of my eyes and that worried me, but then Brandon hooked the ball and started taking it down the field. I was torn. I wanted to make a break for Gerb and tell him to keep it together, but I knew the right thing to do was follow Brandon and make sure that ball made it through the goal. I paused on the field, just for a split second, and then headed for Gerb, trusting that Brandon could bring it home by himself.

Brandon missed the goal. The opposing team took the ball. Gerb got even more agitated when he saw me coming for him, and it was all downhill from there.

They took us out in the last chukker. Gerb got two fouls. Brandon and I didn't score at all, and Baltimore won by five.

This was the farthest any Work to Ride team had ever made it, but we rode off the field feeling like the losers we were.

Afterward, I locked myself into a bathroom stall in the locker room and cried from frustration. We had come so close. I had wanted it so badly. And I was certain that was exactly why we had lost.

———

"Reem? Is that you?"

Bee's voice sounded tinny and thin. I imagined him standing in his tan jumpsuit, using the prison payphone.

I shifted in my seat. "Yeah, bro, hey! I know it's been a minute since we talked. Sorry. The tournament and all that. We been crazy busy."

"That's why I called! Nobody told me what happened. I thought the tournament was like, three days ago. I been waiting to hear!"

I paused for a moment, swallowing the lump in my throat. "Yeah. Well, we got to the second round."

"That's amazing! That's farther than we ever took it before!"

"I know. But you know, we lost to Baltimore. Played crap. Just made a bunch of dumb mistakes."

"How much they win by?"

"Five. We were pretty much tied up to the last chukker."

"Come on! That's not bad at all. Why you sound like someone died?"

"I just . . . it's not fair, Bee. All these teams, they got indoors and fancy ponies and all the time in the world to practice. We got nothing. We got less than nothing. Of course we never gonna win."

Bee snorted. "Well, that's bullshit. You sounding like a whiny little bitch."

I huffed out a laugh. "Come on, I don't . . . I mean, okay, yes. Maybe I'm feeling sorry for myself. But I just wish I could play like you did. The way you could turn a whole game around all on your own."

I could practically hear him roll his eyes. "You think that's the way to captain? I was just running the field like a fool. And let's remember that I never won no championship, either."

I laughed. "That's true." I was quiet for a minute, thinking. "I guess I just wanted it too much."

"Don't be an idiot, Reem. That is the most important thing you got going for you."

"What?"

"You want it—we wanted it—more than any rich white boy ever could. You think those boys really care if they win a trophy? Don't you remember the Hamptons? They got a whole roomful of trophies that nobody looks at except their maid who dusts them off once a week. You bitching about how we got nothing, but that's exactly why we can play like we do. We hungry. We starving compared to those other teams. We eat, sleep, and breathe polo, we want it so bad. Doesn't matter if we don't have an indoor or have to ride a bunch of janky ponies. Remember when we used to stay up all night watching games? Remember how we never talked about anything else but stick and ball?"

"Yeah," I said. "'Course I do."

"That's all you need to win. You gotta want it so bad that there's no room for anything else. The rest will come soon enough."

I smiled. "You sound like Lez. No, wait, you sound like one of those fancy ten-goal coaches screaming at his team."

Bee laughed. Then he got quiet for a minute. "I wish I still wanted anything as much as I wanted that," he finally said. His voice was wistful.

"Bee—" I said.

"I gotta go, bro. There's a line behind me. I keep these guys waiting much longer I'm gonna get shanked."

"Oh. Okay. It was good hearing your voice. Love you. Thanks, man."

"You know it. Love you, too. Say hi to Mom and Lezlie and the fam for me."

—

I sat there for a long time, just staring at the blank screen on my phone after he hung up, imagining him walking back to his cell, lying on his bunk, not being able to see even a sliver of the sky. Wishing so hard that he'd make it out okay.

CHAPTER NINETEEN

Well, this is fucked up." I stared at my phone, looking at the message I had just received.

Gerb looked up from the pony he was brushing. "What?"

"You know Gordon Jones?"

"Um. The quarterback of our school football team? Yeah, I think I might have heard of him."

"He had to quit VF. He lost his scholarship."

"Seriously? He's a senior this year. He was almost done!"

I nodded. "There's more. Guess who yanked the money."

Gerb looked at me. "Really?"

I nodded. "Jones says that Bannerman told him he either had to quit the team or he'd lose the scholarship. But Jones didn't think he'd really do it, so he refused to quit."

Gerb blinked. "Wow. Wasn't Jones getting scouted?"

"Yeah. But he said Bannerman kept insisting that football was a waste of his time and he needed to bring up his grades instead."

Gerb raised his eyebrows. "He knows you riding, right?"

I nodded. "Yeah. I mean, I wasn't really hiding it anymore but it's not that hard to figure out. But I don't think he can tell me to quit since it isn't a school team. Not that he's not trying. Every time we have lunch he spends about an hour talking about what a waste of time polo and horses are."

"Shit, man. Your grades are still good, though, right?"

"Yeah, yeah. They fine, bro."

Gerb looked back down at the pony he was brushing out. "Better keep them that way. Don't want to give that man any excuse."

I nodded again and put my phone away.

—

It was the summer before my senior year, and Gerb and I were back in Lakeville. It was as good as it always was, peaceful, quiet, and balmy, but this summer, we were approaching our work in a new kind of way.

Ever since I'd talked to Bee, I had been trying to figure out where our team was weak and where we were strong. Every day, as I was training the green horses, I'd turn it over in my mind.

We were weak because we didn't have what the other teams had. We didn't have proper practice space, or good horses, or the money to go to camps and clinics. Our gear was worn and mismatched. Our saddles didn't always fit, our boots were secondhand.

We were weak because when we were under pressure we reverted to our worst habits. I couldn't seem to trust that my teammates would play their parts, and that delegation was a good and necessary thing. Gerb couldn't tamp down his righteous and profane anger at the fact that not every call was going to be fair. Brandon had to realize that he was good enough to be more than just a supporting player in the game. Sometimes he should take the lead, too, especially if Gerb and I were shorting out.

We were weak because all through the autumn and winter, we couldn't practice. We didn't have the chance to learn from our mistakes. We had no place to improve our game. We could only change things up on the fly.

We were weak because of our mothers. Tanya was still holding tight on to Brandon, worried sick every time he was out of her sight and she couldn't be sure of his safety. My mother was still using on and off, losing jobs, battling the despair that every new setback brought her. Our concern for them kept us distracted.

We were weak because of Lezlie. We had become too advanced as a team and she cheerfully admitted that sometimes her coaching skills were pushed past their limits. Plus, she couldn't devote herself entirely to just us. She still had to take care of the barn and the horses, the other kids in the program. Money was always short and Work to Ride was in constant crisis. Other teams had ex-pros who were hired for six-figure salaries to do nothing but plan their game strategy and keep the players trained.

We were weak because even now, The Bottom called us back. Brandon was still living on Viola Street, and he faced all the daily danger that came with our neighborhood. Gerb and I still had our family there; David and Bee and Kareema, in and out of jail, Mom and Washika alone in their house, trying to get by. Drea was out there somewhere, and my memories of Mecca. They all had a pull on us. It was easy to imagine any one of the three of us just slipping back in. The Bottom was in our blood and bones.

We were strong because we could ride. We loved horses, and all three of us were at a point where we were as comfortable on horseback as we were on the ground.

We were strong because we were fearless. Bringing on Brandon had changed the whole feel of our team. He was wickedly tenacious and never hesitated to take a risk. We all fed off of each other's confidence, supporting each other as we tried for bigger moves and better plays.

We were strong because between the hand-me-down horses at the barn and the green colts we were riding all summer, it was nothing for us to jump on a pony we'd never ridden before and ride it to a win. Everyone always said that in polo, a rider is only as good as their pony, and that was definitely true, but when we were playing, we had no choice but to ride whoever we were given. Some of the teams we played actually brought their own string of ponies along with them rather than use the horses that the schools or clubs provided. We played whatever horse we were offered, so we had no time to figure out which horse was the fastest or needed babying. We just had to saddle up and go. But learning on ponies like Angel and then Buck, getting thrown off, training a horse like Cholo, knowing how to calm young and quirky and sensitive colts, and inspire a listless pony to pick up its heels, gave us a huge advantage when we were handed a string of ponies we'd never ridden before. We could take just about any horse and make them run.

We were strong because we never had the home advantage. We didn't have an indoor where we could host games, so we were always on someone else's turf. But that meant we could be comfortable almost anywhere. We had learned to play on a mangy soccer field and a pasture full of cow shit and wallows. Any club and arena felt like a manicured golf course compared to that.

We were strong because of our mothers. Lazette and Tanya might have raised us in different ways and made different kinds of parenting choices, but they both ended up with confident, accomplished children who were working hard to figure it all out. Brandon's mom had protected him and given him the time and space to be a kid and not worry about too much, too soon. My mom had taught us to look our fears in the face and stare them down.

We were strong because of Lezlie. Having a coach who loved you like a mother might be a little embarrassing sometimes, but I'd realized that her warm encouragement and pride was worth a hundred ten-goal coaches screaming out plays and berating their teams for not doing what they were told. Lezlie had given her life over to us and the barn; there was nothing she wouldn't do to see us succeed. Without her, we might just be kids on the street, with no particular future in sight. Lezlie shaped our lives, she taught us to work and play, she brought us once-in-a-lifetime opportunities and then made sure we followed through on them. She gave us horses. And because we loved her just as fiercely as she loved us, we worked as hard as we could to make her proud.

We were strong because the three of us had known each other from the time we were little kids toddling around Viola Street. There was a shorthand between us. I could glance at Gerb's face and have a pretty good idea what he was thinking. Gerb and Brandon had always been attached at the hip and could practically complete each other's sentences. We had spent thousands of hours hanging out, getting into trouble, and now riding together. This was something I couldn't imagine that any of the teams we played against had. We were brothers, through blood and choice, and that made us tighter than any team I knew.

We were strong because of The Bottom. We'd spent our whole lives being told to get out, to turn away from the hood and never come back if we were given the chance; but our home made us hungry, and that hunger made us succeed. We were strong because our neighborhood had given us real, life-or-death reasons to win.

I'd told Bee that we were never going to be champions because we had nothing, that we were at an impossible disadvantage, that it wasn't fair; but when I laid it all out like this, I could see how wrong I'd been.

Our work that summer was to correct whatever we could before we started playing again that fall. I was an incoming senior. This was our last chance to play as a team and take the prize. I was determined to figure out how to use what we had and get around the things we didn't.

Gerb and I spent every extra second we had that summer riding and playing together. We always stuck close in Lakeville, but I wanted us to leave Connecticut that year with the connection between us more powerful than it had ever been. I wanted to instinctively recognize every look that passed over my brother's face. I wanted to sense when he was going to turn right or left or power forward before he even made a move. I wanted to know all his tells, his quirks, his bad habits on the field. I wanted to be sure that we could pass messages to each other without a word spoken between us. And I needed him to be able to recognize all the same things in me.

The way to make that happen was the same way you trained a green pony—do it over and over again until it was muscle memory. Then do it some more until it was so automatic that it felt like pure instinct. So that was what we did. We played the way that Mecca and I used to run the streets, keeping at it until the sun went down and our eyes could barely stay open, and we were so tired we thought we might drop right where we were standing.

By the time we left Lakeville that year, I was determined that we'd be able to read each other's minds.

—

"You think we ever gonna have a place like this for our own, Reem?"

We were in our beds in our Lakeville room. I could hear the buzz and song of cicadas and crickets outside our windows. A breeze blew through the screens, bringing in the scent of sweet hay, night-blooming flowers, and the earthier smell of the ponies. There was a pale silver wash of moonlight on the floor. The darkness that surrounded the edges of light was soft and comforting to me. I realized with a small laugh that I actually liked the dark now; it didn't scare me anymore.

"Maybe," I answered. "I hope so."

"It's just like we imagined it when we were kids, right? A big old farmhouse, the ponies and the stables and the barn?"

I yawned and stretched, touching my toes to the base of my bed. "Needs the fam, though."

"Bee would love it here," said Gerb.

"They all would," I agreed.

"Maybe not Washika."

We laughed. Our beautiful baby sister had turned out to

be terrified of horses. She'd taken one ride at the barn and then declared she was never going to come back again.

"She doesn't have to ride," I said. "She could just hang out with Mom on the front porch, bossing us around."

We were quiet for a moment, listening to the insects sing, the occasional night bird calling.

"Think this will be your last time here?" asked Gerb.

I nodded slowly. "Probably," I said. "I'm going to have to get a job that pays more before I go away for college, but Mark said he'd be happy to have you and Brandon next year if you want to come back."

"That would be cool," said Gerb. "Not the same, but still cool."

"Sure." I yawned.

"Hard to imagine coming back here without you, though."

"We'll have a place like this for our own one day," I said, deciding to make it true. "We can bring our kids and they can share a room just like we do and your kid will talk too fucking much and keep my kid from going to sleep."

Gerb chuckled. "Good night, bro."

"Yup. You, too."

CHAPTER TWENTY

I just don't see how horses fit into your future, Cadet. Polo is a rich man's game."

Another lunch, another lecture. I tried my hardest to let Bannerman's words wash over me and not take his bait, but ever since Gordon Jones had lost his scholarship, I felt like I'd better start paying more attention.

"Respectfully, I wouldn't be here without polo, sir."

Bannerman shook his head. "You wouldn't be here without my money."

I bit the inside of my cheek to keep myself from saying something I'd regret. "That is also true, sir. And I am extremely grateful for your generosity."

He took a sip of his martini. "So you're spending every weekend at games?"

"Yes, sir."

"And you don't think that affects your GPA?"

"My last report card was a 3.8, sir."

"But it could be a 4.0."

I looked down at the remains of the pasta that sat in front of me. "I don't think any amount of time is going to change the fact that I find AP biochemistry to be a bit difficult, sir."

"You're not going to get better at anything if you don't work at it, Cadet."

"I fully agree, sir."

He took the last bite of his sandwich and chewed with an absent look on his face. "Okay, let's try this. What is it you like so much about this silly game?"

I took a drink of water to cover up my surprise. He'd never bothered to ask before.

It saved my life, I thought. *More than once.*

But I wasn't going to say that to him.

"It is a misunderstood game, sir. I don't mean to contradict you, but there is nothing silly about it."

He snorted. "Golf on horseback? Seems pretty ridiculous to me."

"It takes a lot of skill and strength, sir. It is also extremely dangerous."

He whacked his hand against the table. "This is exactly what I'm talking about. All the more reason not to play! Why endanger yourself for something so insubstantial?"

Just join a military academy and enlist instead, I thought. *No danger there.*

I took a deep breath. "Have you ever actually seen a game, sir?"

He frowned. "No. Never wanted to."

"Have you ridden horses, sir?"

He rolled his eyes. "Not my thing."

Fine.

I took a deep breath. "It helps me sleep, sir." I blurted it out quickly.

He wrinkled his forehead. "What do you mean?"

"Polo helps me sleep, sir. If I don't ride, I find that I have a difficult time sleeping."

"Sleeping."

"Yes, sir." That was as much as I could bring myself to tell him.

He squinted at me. "Any vigorous exercise would help with insomnia, Cadet. You could just take a run around the campus and I'm sure you'd sleep like a baby."

I shook my head. "I have found that it has to be horses, sir."

"There is medication you could take for that. You don't have to take a pony ride just to get some sleep."

"I think I do, sir."

He scratched his head. Picked up his glass and then put it down again. "You're a frustrating kid, Cadet."

"I'd be happy for you to come see me play anytime you like, sir."

He lifted his hand as if he was shooing away a fly. "Not my thing," he said again.

"Yes, sir."

The waiter stopped by with the check. Bannerman handed him his credit card.

He looked me in the eyes. "Just don't let me down, Cadet."

I nodded, my eyes straight ahead in military posture. "Yes, sir. I know, sir."

———

That fall was cold and wet. The leaves turned early that year. We tried to get as much practice in as possible while we could still play outside, but one morning, much earlier than I expected, I woke up and there were four inches of snow blanketing the VF campus.

Once winter came, that was the end of our practice season. We couldn't ride our horses on ice and snow—too dangerous for both the pony and the rider. Lezlie semi-shut down the barn in the winter. She made sure it was snug and warm, and invited kids in to clean stalls and groom and braid manes and tails and be around the horses, even if we couldn't ride them.

The snow didn't stop us from traveling, though. We had a game in Maryland, so Lezlie strapped on her snow chains and we headed down south.

We won. Just like we had won all our games so far that season. Gerb and I had come back from Connecticut almost perfectly in sync, and with his crazy capacity to learn things just about twice as fast as anyone else could, it took Brandon no time at all to join us. From the moment we hit the field, it was like a ballet, we moved around each other so well. We started playing on another level. I could look at Gerb's face from across the field and know exactly what move he was going to make. I would see Brandon just slightly flex his right arm and know precisely where he was planning on hitting the ball. They could both look at me and then immediately get into the formation we had talked about before the game. I found myself relaxing my vigilance. They didn't need me to play for them when they were playing like pros on their own. I finally realized that we each had our parts and when we were allowed to perform them, we won.

The scrimmage had ended late, so Lezlie decided to get

motel rooms for the night and drive back to Philly in the morning.

"Okay, you guys," I said, pulling out my laptop once Lezlie was asleep in her room and we were sprawled out in ours. "Come here."

"What is it?" asked Gerb. "Porn?"

"Hilarious," I said.

I pulled up the window I wanted and hit play. "The Argentine Open, 1986."

Gerb got a big, goofy grin on his face. "The O.G.'s," he said. "The Heguy brothers!"

Brandon crowded closer, squinting at the screen. "Cool. I haven't seen this game before."

We watched for a minute, marveling at how well the game was being played. Then I hit pause.

"Okay, so, we can't practice anymore, but we can watch the hell out these old games. We can watch them and talk them through and then steal as many of their moves as we possibly can."

"To stealing!" said Brandon, lifting the paper cup he'd found in the bathroom.

"Yo, I'm serious," I said. "If we can't practice, we have to find a path to improve in other ways. The Heguys are genius-level players. There is no reason why we can't learn their formations and tricks and then apply them to our own games."

"Sounds like homework," said Gerb.

"It *is* homework, bro. I wish we could all just hang out on the living-room floor with a bag of Doritos and watch these games together like we used to, but we don't have time. We got to watch them on our own and then come back together and discuss."

"But tonight we can watch together," said Gerb.

"Yes," I said. "I found a bunch of them."

"No chips, though," said Brandon.

I pointed at the door. "There's a vending machine in the lobby."

—

We stayed up late, eating plastic-wrapped snacks and watching the games. Trying to absorb all the tricks and moves, pausing and pointing and trying to deconstruct how the great players pulled off their wins. Every time we saw something particularly clever, I would pause and rewind and we'd watch it over and over until we understood what they were doing and had completely committed their moves to memory.

On the way back up to Philly, trying to drown out the sounds of Terry Gross interviewing Aaron Sorkin on the radio, we talked about everything we had watched the night before, debating what we thought we were capable of and how we could bring it into our own game. Once in a while, Lezlie would even turn down *Fresh Air* and add in her opinion.

When we weren't talking, I closed my eyes and ran games in my head. Not just the ones we'd watched, but ones we'd played, ones I *wanted* to play. Maybe we didn't have an indoor, but that didn't mean we had to stop practicing the game.

Over the next weeks, separately and together, we came back to those games, and any others we could find, dozens of times. I set up an old VCR and TV in my dorm room and Gerb and I would grab whatever time we had before reveille to work our way through Lezlie's pile of tapes. Brandon was doing the same at his place. Every time we were together we dissected what we had seen. If we couldn't practice on the field, we were going to practice the only way we could.

—

"If you can get into Cornell, you can get into West Point."

"Respectfully, sir, I do not want to go to West Point."

"Annapolis, then."

"I do not want to continue in the military, sir."

"Why? Because you'd have to give up polo?"

"That is one of the reasons, sir."

"Continuing your education at a military academy would open all sorts of doors for you. It would assure your future."

"I feel that polo has also opened doors for me, sir."

"Cadet, do you actually think you're going to be a professional polo player?"

"No, sir. I have other plans. But I need to keep playing as well."

"You are making a mistake."

"I hope not, sir."

"You understand that I am telling you this for your own good, right? You know that I wouldn't bother if I didn't care?"

"I do, sir, and I appreciate that."

"But you're still not going to take my advice? You're not going to apply to a military academy?"

"No, sir. I am not."

He swiped his hand over his face, frustrated. "All right. Obviously I can't force you." He signed the bill. "Have a good day, Cadet."

"You, too, sir. Thank you for lunch."

"Cadet?"

"Yes, sir."

"Don't let me down."

I nodded. "Yes, sir."

———

"One . . . two . . . three! We're not going to lose today!"

We shouted out those words just before every game that season. Looking back, it makes me laugh. I'm sure anyone who overheard us thought we were crazy. No, "Go team!" or "Victory!" or even just, "We're going to win!"

"We're not going to lose today!"

We said it because, despite our recent streak of good luck, after all the years of setbacks, all those years of defeat, losing had begun to feel like a habit, a fallback position, an expectation. We chanted it to break the curse and change our story.

And it worked. We didn't lose. We played game after game and took every win. The chemistry was there. We were clicking. We were running the plays that we had planned out in our heads. We got to a level where we hardly spoke to each other on the field at all. We could just read each other's body language. We used to yell across the field as we played, but now, we were communicating through movement. It was a flow, an altered state. I've heard other athletes call this feeling grace or transcendence—the moment when you are playing at such a high level with your team that you are all of one mind. Even the ponies seemed to know what we wanted before we could ask.

Honestly, it sometimes felt like magic. We played both high-school-level clubs and colleges, and we were beating them all by miles. We were unstoppable. We racked up win after win, wearing our shitty boots and ragged uniforms, laughing our asses off in delight as we got closer and closer to the final goal. We won the regionals. And then, finally, at last, we were first seed and undefeated and set to play the championship. Our final game was in Virginia, against the team we had lost to the year before, the Baltimore Polo Club.

—

"What if you get hurt? What if you fall off a horse and break your neck?"

"It's a risk, sir. Playing any sport could end that way."

"But you told me that polo is particularly dangerous."

"Yes, sir. It can be. I happen to feel that the benefits outweigh the risk."

He practically growled. "Don't you throw risk-benefit ratios at me, Cadet. Do you know what I do for a living?"

"Yes, sir. If it makes you feel any better, sir, I am a very strong rider."

He waved his hand in the air. "You kids, you think a little athletic talent means you're all going to end up being Joe Namath. Don't you know how shortsighted that is?"

I bit my lip to hide my smile. "I truly don't think I'm Joe Namath, sir."

He glared at me. Threw his napkin down. "That's enough for today." He called the waitress over. "Wrap up his food. He'll take it with him."

"Sir?"

"What?"

"The team I captain, we made the finals. We are ranked first seed. We have a very good chance of winning the national championship this year, sir, and we'd be the first all African American team to do so."

He was quiet. Waiting.

"I thought maybe you would like to attend the tournament? I have tickets I could—"

"No thank you, Cadet."

I blinked. "Okay. I just thought maybe—"

"I'm very busy."

I swallowed. "Of course, sir."

The waitress brought me my leftovers wrapped in foil.

"Thank you for lunch, sir."

He nodded. "Good luck with your game."

"Thank you, sir."

He met my eyes. "Don't let me down, Cadet."

CHAPTER TWENTY-ONE

My mom and Washika were moving out of the house on Viola Street. They would still be in West Philly, but now that most of her kids were out of the house, my mom had found a place that was a little smaller and cheaper.

We were a week away from our tournament. We didn't have any games that weekend, but I'd taken leave anyway so I could come back and help my mom move.

It was funny, but when it came to Washika, my mom had changed her parenting style. Maybe it was because she was more grown up by the time Washika came along, but my mother parented her youngest child much like Tanya parented Brandon, paying more attention, being more careful, keeping her child close and behind doors. Washika was never allowed to run wild like we had done. My mom claimed it was because the neighborhood had gotten worse over the years. She felt that she used to be able to depend upon her neighbors to report back to her if her kids were in trouble, or help them out if they were in a jam, but now, she said, everyone only seemed to be in it for themselves. She wasn't wrong. Crime rates had gone up. There were more guns, more drugs, more violence, more poverty. There was a new drift of fear in The Bottom that hadn't been there when I was a kid. The sense of community we used to feel on our block had fragmented into something harder and uglier.

Mom was mostly packed up when I arrived. She didn't have much. A dining-room table and some chairs, a couple of mattresses, some boxes of clothes and Washika's toys, some photos and kitchen stuff. Despite the packing mess, the house was, as usual, just-scrubbed and eat-off-the-floor clean.

She was doing better lately. The late-night phone calls had slowed down and she was back in NA. She said this move was a fresh start.

The place felt strange emptied out, and I felt strange realizing that it was probably the last time I'd ever be inside its walls again. It had never been much. It was owned by a slumlord who did only the minimum work to keep it from being condemned, but it had been my family home for my whole childhood, and the last place where all six of us kids and my mom had been under the same roof.

Since I'd started at Valley Forge, I came back to the barn as often as I could, but I rarely made it home to Viola Street. I saw my mom, and talked to her on the phone all the time, but the house had stopped feeling like mine a long while back. So I was surprised to feel such a wave of sadness about getting ready to empty it out and close it up.

I was the only kid home. Washika was off with a cousin. Gerb had stayed at VF to catch up on some homework. David and Bee were both in prison at this point; Bee had just started a four-year sentence and David was two years into his six. Kareema had a court date coming up for sentencing. She would end up going in for a shorter stint.

I carried some of the boxes out to the car my mom had borrowed to transport her stuff. We puzzled over how we were going to get the table to fit, until I realized that we'd have to take off the legs.

"Let me fix you a plate first," said my mom. "While the table's still standing."

She went into the kitchen and pulled out the few things that she had left in the fridge, making us each a sandwich and some salad, which she put on paper plates with plastic cutlery. We sat down at the table.

It actually felt nice for it to be just me and her for once. Usually when we got together, at least Washika and Gerb were around, too.

"You nervous about the tournament?" she asked, picking at her salad.

I bit into my sandwich, wondering why home food always tasted better, even if it was just thrown together.

"A little, I guess," I said with my mouth full. It was shocking how fast I forgot the VF mess-hall rules when I was at my mom's kitchen table. I swallowed. "Stupid not to be."

"Way you boys been playing lately, I don't guess there's much chance you're going to lose."

I raised my eyebrows. "I hope you're right."

"Wish I could be there."

I shrugged. "You got work. I get it. Don't want you to lose your job just to see us play."

"At least you'll have Lez, anyway."

I looked at her. There wasn't even a hint of bitterness in her tone. Sometimes it still surprised me that she truly seemed to have no jealousy at all about Lezlie's role in our lives. They didn't always see eye to eye on everything, and there had been more than a few arguments over the years, but my mom absolutely accepted Lezlie's importance to us all. In fact, she was grateful for it, she'd told me. She didn't care what people said about her letting a white lady into our business. It wasn't easy raising six kids on her own, and Lezlie had stepped in and taken up some of the burden.

She reached over and patted my hand. "I'm real proud of you, Reem."

I squeezed her hand back. "Thanks, Mom."

"I haven't done much with my life, but I made you kids. You all are the best part of me."

She meant it, too. She kept a scrapbook of every newspaper article about Work to Ride, every good report card Gerb and I sent home. Every prize we'd ever won. She'd already told me she was going to buy a set of shelves for the new house where she could put the trophy she was sure we were bringing home from Virginia next week.

I watched her as we finished eating. She was still young, still beautiful. Sometimes she talked about how, now that her kids were almost all grown up, she'd finally have the time to figure out what she wanted to be when *she* grew up. She talked about maybe finishing high school. She still wanted that little house with some land out in the country. She wanted to move to a small town in New Jersey or rural Pennsylvania. She liked to imagine the garden she'd grow.

After all these years, she hadn't given up; she was still thinking about how to get out.

"Guess we better get this table apart," I said after we finished our food. I wondered just how we were going to do that. Neither of us was mechanically inclined and we probably didn't have anything better to use than the edge of a spoon to get the screws out.

"You're a good boy to come and help your mother," she said, giving me her dazzling smile.

I smiled back at her, but there was a piece of me that wanted to cry.

—

Lezlie wasn't in the barn when I stopped by the next morning. There was a volunteer out in the ring with a couple of kids, but the stables were mostly quiet. I grabbed a bag of horse treats and wandered up and down the stalls, handing out some cookies and seeing which horses were around. Before I even got to his stall, Cholo was whinnying hello.

"Hey there, boy," I said as I offered him a treat. He peeled back his lips and used his front teeth to delicately take the biscuit from the palm of my hand.

"You still cooped up in here?" I asked him. His messy stall showed signs of him not being turned out yet.

I didn't know when Lezlie would get back so I figured I'd make myself useful. I slipped the halter over Cholo's head and led him out into the back corral, turning him out with a few other horses I knew he liked. I watched him for a second, laughing at the way he picked up a trot as soon as he saw a mare that I knew he was into. Then I grabbed a pitchfork and went back to his stall to clean.

Shoveling shit and adding bedding to a stall used to be the

thing I hated most about working in a barn, but as I got older and stronger and the work became both easier and more automatic, I'd started to enjoy the mindlessness of it. As soon as I picked up a pitchfork, my brain basically went on automatic. It was probably the closest I ever got to meditation, and I always got a small thrill when I finished and the stall was clean and the sawdust was perfectly evened off, just waiting for the horse to come back in and mess it all up again.

After I wheeled the dirty bedding out to the manure pile and put the pitchfork and shovel away, Lezlie sent me a message saying that she wouldn't be in for another couple hours. So I went back to the corral and whistled for Cholo, who came running just like I'd taught him to.

I rubbed the star on his forehead and passed him another cookie and then put the halter back on and led him into the barn. There had been a warm spell the past few days, and the snow had melted off the bridle paths in the park. I thought I'd do a little hacking with my horse.

Lezlie had recently asked me if I was ready to sell Cholo yet, since I'd be going to college soon and would probably need the money, but I'd told her no, that I wanted him to stay. I liked the idea of my horse being here, even when I couldn't be. He would've made a great polo pony, but I think he was happier in the barn, teaching kids to ride.

I tightened the girth around his belly and slid off his halter and replaced it with his bridle. I'd fished out a helmet and an old pair of my boots from the tack room, so I was geared up well enough.

Fairmount Park felt endless. You could ride all day and still not cover all of it. We started at the racetrack, as we called it, the long, wide stretch of path where Black Cowboys from our hood would come and race their horses and make bets. Sometimes Bee, Gerb, and I would sneak our ponies down here and do some of our own racing. Bee always won, of course.

Apparently Cholo was excited to get out of the ring and into the woods, because he was trotting along at a nice clip. I laughed to myself thinking that if Cholo had been around when we'd been racing, I would have definitely won a race or two.

We passed a playground where Kareema and I had once had the bright idea to charge for pony rides without asking Lezlie. We'd taken Arquetta down here and led her around, offering kids a ride for five bucks a pop. We made twenty-five dollars before Lezlie found us and forced us to give the money back. She was so mad. She told us we were lucky nobody got hurt and ended up suing the barn.

We turned deeper into the park at a corner where I'd stood, shivering, one day with Gerb and Bee, holding up a cardboard sign soliciting donations for the barn so the passing traffic could see it. Lezlie had come in that morning white-lipped and desperate. Our funds were so low she couldn't even afford to feed the horses. She'd sent us out with our signs and we'd stood there, miserable, until enough sympathetic horse lovers had stopped their cars and handed us cash to buy some hay.

I brought Cholo up to an easy canter when we got to the place where Mecca and I had turned off the path and raced through the woods the morning after we'd first spent the night in the barn. I could practically see the two of us, hand in hand, Mecca's braids flying behind her, disappearing into the twist of winter-bare trees and undergrowth.

Sometimes I wondered what would have happened if David and Bee had turned right instead of left on their bikes that day. Would we have found the barn another time? Probably we would have, eventually—we were always exploring the park—but it might have been too late. My brothers might have been older and too cool to admit they actually wanted to ride a pony. We might have laughed at the Black kids on horses, talked about how mean-looking that white lady was, and then never come back.

I don't know who I would have been without the barn.

There were only a few times and places in my life where I had felt like I was truly content just to be myself. Ever since I was a little kid, I'd spent a lot of my time trying or wishing to be somebody I really wasn't. I'd felt like I needed to protect my mother; I wished myself bigger and more threatening to keep her safe. With my big brothers out on the streets, I'd always felt like I needed to be more like them, tougher and braver and more reckless than I actually was. Even when I was at the barn, I wanted to be good, follow the rules, make Lezlie happy. At the polo clubs and the Hamptons and Connecticut, I did my best not to show anyone just how overwhelmed I was by all the rules of wealth and society. Of course, when I went away to Valley Forge, my code-switching reached an all-time high; I had the individuality beaten out of me as a plebe, so I had one voice with the staff, another with the ranked cadets, and something else with the shit bags, and I sounded like a new person entirely during my lunches with Bannerman.

Only with Mecca had I dropped my various personas and felt exactly right in my own skin. And only riding Cholo did I reach the point where my self-consciousness dissolved so completely that I had no thoughts at all about who I was supposed to be.

On the horse that I trained, riding through the park that I loved, I simply was.

CHAPTER TWENTY-TWO

We drove down the night before the tournament, piling into Lezlie's car, Gerb and Brandon shoulder to shoulder, sleeping in the backseat, me in the front, Lezlie at the wheel.

I meant to run plays in my head, going over the thousands of possibilities we might encounter on the field the next day, preparing myself for anything that could happen, but it was late and the car was warm and dark.

Instead, I rested my forehead against the window, watching the headlights flow past us in the other direction, and let my mind drift where it wanted.

I thought about the Argentine polo families with their ten-goal dynasties. The way a father put his son onto his first pony and handed him a tiny mallet and created his child's destiny before he could even walk.

I thought about the way our mom would hand us each a bottle of soda on really hot nights and lead us out onto our front porch so we could watch what was happening in the street instead of just listening to it from our dark, stuffy room while we tried to fall asleep.

I thought about the mural on North 39th Street. I wondered if my father ever walked past it and whether he had any idea that his sons were painted up there, three stories high.

I thought about the family team. How it used to be me, David, and Bee. Then me, Bee, and Gerb. Then we added Mecca. And now Brandon. How Brandon had become family to me, too.

I thought about a paper I still had to write for my poli-sci class. Whether we won the championship or not, I'd need to get it started by Monday or I'd end up turning it in late.

I thought about the pretty girl with a big, wide smile and a red T-shirt who had passed by on the street while I was helping my mom pack up her car.

I thought about how it would feel to hold the trophy. I laughed when I thought about how it might piss off some people to see our names, Kareem and Daymar, etched into the metal alongside all the Bradley Smith-Worthington IIIs that I was pretty sure were already on it.

I wondered how it would feel to win.

I wondered if I would cry.

I thought about David and Bee. My brilliant, talented brothers. I thought about how sometimes it felt like they had been taken, disappeared, stolen from me just as unfairly as Mecca had been. I wondered how they managed to survive in a place where there were no horses.

When we won (because I was certain we would) I wondered if anyone would dare to call it dumb luck, or smile and wink and congratulate us on our heart or grit or whatever mealy word you use when you're describing the scrappy little underdogs who managed to fall backward into their win. I wondered if winning the championship would finally end the feeling that we were some sideshow act come to add a little bit of literal color to the endless sea of money and privilege and whiteness that we'd been playing in for years.

I thought about breakfast. We'd stayed at this motel before and they had a good breakfast bar. I was hoping it would be open before we had to leave for the tournament. I decided I would have the pancakes.

—

That night, after everyone was asleep, my phone rang. I stepped out of our room into the hallway as I glanced down to see who was calling.

My mother, of course.

My heart sank. I didn't think I had it in me to do a phone call like this on that particular night. What if she wasn't sober? She'd just managed to get clean.

I almost didn't answer. I didn't want to listen to her cry.

I knew I could text her in the morning. Make an excuse for not picking up. Say I was asleep or the battery had died in my phone. But then I thought about her, awake in her new house while Washika slept. The place had been small and kind of grim. The neighborhood was even worse than Viola Street. I wasn't sure what kind of fresh start she was really going to get there. I imagined her sitting there, all the unpacked boxes around her. I knew that she was lonely. She needed someone to talk to.

"Mom?" I said.

"Oh, Reem," she said. "I didn't think you were going to pick up. Why aren't you asleep, baby?"

I shook my head. "Well, I almost was," I said. "But some-one called my phone."

She laughed softly. "Sorry."

I relaxed a little. I could tell from her voice she wasn't high.

"Everything okay?" I asked.

"Yes, yes," she said. Her tone of voice was low, almost a croon, and suddenly I remembered a time when I was little and had the flu; how she had tested my forehead for a fever with the back of her hand, and then, after giving me an aspirin and a glass of water, she'd lain down beside me and kept me company until I fell asleep.

"Everything's fine, baby," she said. "I just thought I'd wish you good luck on your voicemail, but then you actually picked up the phone."

"Well," I said. "You could go ahead and say it now instead."

She laughed again. "That so?"

I rolled my eyes. "Mom, it's almost midnight."

"Boy!" she said, teasing. "Where's the respect for your elders?"

I sighed. "Mom—"

"Okay, okay," she said. "Good luck, Reem. Get that championship. I know you guys are gonna do great." Her voice shook a little. "You tell your brother, I'm so proud of you both. I love you so much."

"Thanks, Mom," I said. "I love you, too."

She started crying after that, but this time, I didn't mind.

—

We dressed carefully. Our whites were pressed, our jerseys were pristine, our belts and boots were clean and polished.

We groomed our horses, brushing them until they shined, but also taking the time to run our fingers over their spines and legs, checking their hooves, making sure they were absolutely sound.

It was already clean, but we cleaned our tack again, scrubbing and polishing, checking all the buckles and ties, making sure nothing was going to snap or break midway through the game.

We tacked up our first ponies: pad, saddle, stirrups, girth. We double-checked everything and then made sure that our bridles were ready and waiting.

After we finished, I looked at Gerb and Brandon. "C'mon," I said. "We still got some time. Let's go out to the field."

It wasn't good for us just to stand around waiting. We needed a distraction.

We squinted in the bright sun as we emerged from the barn, heading for the vast, green field that stood untouched and ready for the summer polo season. Unable to resist, I threw myself down on the manicured grass.

"Bro, that was a big mistake. You're gonna stain your jeans," said Gerb, laughing at me lying on the ground.

I pillowed my arms behind my head. "Naw, man, the ground is dry. Come on. It feels good."

My teammates gingerly lowered themselves to the ground, and then, after ascertaining it was safe, stretched out on their backs on either side of me.

We were quiet for a minute, just taking deep breaths and staring up at the pale blue sky.

Finally Brandon spoke. "What if we fuck up today?"

I laughed. "That's not going to happen."

Gerb popped back up. "But what if we do?"

I kept my eyes on the sky. "We can't. This is it. Last chance. After this, I'm graduating and we done."

Brandon sat up, too. "Yo, how is that supposed to make us feel any better?"

I shook my head. "Listen. All we have to do is go out on that field, play like we been playing all season, and in twenty-eight minutes, everything will have changed. We got this. We can finish. I don't have a doubt in my mind."

Brandon and Gerb were quiet. I watched a crow circle in the sky.

"What do you think Lez will do if we win?" said Brandon.

"Cry," said Gerb and I together.

"She cry at anything," said Brandon. "She cried when we were watching a cat-food commercial the other day."

"She already cried her eyes out when she found out we were even going this far," I said.

Gerb turned toward me. "Yeah, but can you blame her? I mean, I can't even believe we actually here. It's finally happening. I keep thinking about it, but it just don't feel real."

I looked over at him. "It's real," I said. "We here. Remember it. Enjoy it." I turned my head back to the sky and smiled to myself. "Because bro, we sure did fucking earn it."

———

Before we counted off and chanted, *"We're not going to lose today,"* before I swung up onto my first pony of the game, before we rode out onto the field, before the ump bowled in the ball, before I pulled back my mallet and hit that ball with all the pent-up force of ten years of waiting for this moment—before all that—I walked to the edge of the arena and looked out over the stadium.

The ponies were being hot-walked, the umps were riding the ring, the bleachers were full of chattering people, but none of our folk were there in the audience. We didn't have a fan in the seats or know a single soul watching.

Sometimes when you're the first of your kind to do something, it can feel like the loneliest thing. When you are the first to walk through a door where people like you have not been welcome before, it can be very hard not to feel like you'll always be alone in that room.

But of course, I wasn't alone. I had Brandon and Gerb and Lezlie—we broke that boundary together—but I also had David and Bee and Kareema and Drea and Mecca with me; they'd all led me to this place.

I wasn't so special. It could have been any of them. It *should* have been them. I was only standing where I was standing because people left or were dragged away or were discarded and lost and couldn't be retrieved.

I was only there because of luck and chance and because I honestly needed it to survive.

I was only there because my big brothers decided to go for a bike ride on a misty autumn day.

I took a deep breath.

It was nearly time.

—

I wish the story of our final game was more dramatic.

I wish I could tell you that it was a game more like the one we'd played the year before—that we traded goals back and forth up until the very last moment, and then I managed to hook the ball and hit it to Brandon, who hit it to Gerb, who made a pony shot right between the goal posts just as the last seconds counted down on the clock. I wish I had another two-point foul shot I managed to make at just the right moment, or maybe that someone's horse had rolled, but the rider got right back up and made the winning shot and no one realized until after the game was over that they'd actually been playing with a broken arm.

But this game—our championship game—was not any of those things. In fact, I'm just going to tell you right up front: we rode out onto the field, just like we had been doing all season, immediately took the lead, never lost it, dominated the game, and then, we won.

—

Here's what the game actually was, though.

The game was poetry. Military. Music. We never missed a step.

We were young kings. We were brothers. We were those kids on Viola Street, playing stick and ball with our mother's stolen broomstick and an empty plastic water bottle. We were the sound of metal horseshoes clanging on the pavement as the Black Cowboys charged down the street. We were my mother's desperate cries for help. We were my father trying to drink himself to death in that empty lot. We were the feeling you get when the police beat down your door.

We were Mecca's boots, backward in the stirrups, being carried toward the church.

We were David leading me around the ring. We were Kareema, her fingers flying as she weaved a ribbon through a pony's tail. We were Tanya, tenderly watching over three small boys as they slept beneath her roof. We were the sweet sound of Washika's laugh. We were Drea, slamming his fist into someone's jaw.

We were Bee, raising his mallet over his head in triumph as he flew down the field.

We were Angel and Buck, Arquetta and Buddha and Perfect Rhythm. We were Cholo teaching a little girl to ride.

We were Lezlie, inviting us into the barn for the very first time.

We were the first African-American polo team ever to win the National Interscholastic Championship.

We were filled with wonder and joy and the pure, sweet knowledge that we had finally showed everyone just who we really were.

We were the champions. We were the family team.

EPILOGUE

After the championship, I graduated with honors from Valley Forge. With financial help from Work to Ride I attended Colorado State University, where I led their polo team to a national championship. Their first in sixteen years. I was named both Interscholastic and Intercollegiate Player of the Year.

I graduated from CSU with a major in economics. I was the first in my family to get a college degree.

After college, even though I had been told my whole life that if I ever got out, I should never come back, I came back to Philly. It is my home and always will be.

I don't live in The Bottom anymore. I have a job in finance and an apartment in Washington Square. Every night I sit with my two cats and watch the sun set over the city from my window.

—

My family still lives in West Philadelphia. I spend a lot of time thinking about how I can help them get out.

My mom and Washika still live together. Washika graduated high school and is applying to culinary school. Bee was let out of prison more than five years ago and has stayed out since. He has a son, Jabarr Jr.

Kareema lives not too far from our mom, with her three beautiful kids, Ukkashar, Maryam, and Abdullah. She is an amazing mother to her children, one that our mother says she learns from every day.

Gerb graduated from Roger Williams University, where he helped found their first polo team. That team and Gerb went on to win the intercollegiate championship the following year. Gerb also returned to Philly. He is now working as a marketing coordinator.

Brandon's mother Tanya passed away from liver failure in 2018. Brandon dropped out of college. He is currently driving for Lyft and Uber and has started his own business.

Drea is still in prison. He has a daughter.

———

When I returned home from college, the barn was faltering and Lezlie's health was not at its best. I thought about what I could do to help, and then I offered to take over the financial end of Work to Ride. I became the executive director of the nonprofit fundraising arm called Friends of Work to Ride. So far, we have raised more than $800,000 for the barn, and I have secured a partnership with Polo Ralph Lauren to support the Work to Ride foundation with a grant that directly funds collegiate scholarships for the Work to Ride high-school athletes. Gerb and I and other Work to Ride students were featured prominently on the brand's website. We continue to model for them still.

I will not rest until Work to Ride has the kind of endowment that will keep it safe and solvent forever.

Our next project at the barn is to build an indoor riding ring.

—

I am still riding and playing polo every chance I get.

—

When I began to write this book, I asked Bee if he would sit down with me. For the very first time we really talked about what happened, why he left.

He told me he wished he was still playing. He wished that we still were on the same team.

I laughed. "The family team?"

"Sure," he said. "Why not? The family team."

It makes me so happy to see him wanting something again. It is my dearest wish to make that team a reality.

—

After a happy lifetime of throwing kids off his back, Buck peacefully passed on several years ago.

Cholo is alive and well and still teaching children to ride at the barn. He changes lives every single day.

—

On March 11, 2020, as I was finishing up the final edits on this book, my brother David Raheem Rosser was murdered. He was shot on the street, in broad daylight, multiple times in the abdomen and twice in the head. He passed away at Penn Presbyterian Medical Center the next morning at 8:03 A.M. His organs were donated to help other people survive.

I don't know why he was killed. I don't know if it was someone from his past who came back to find him, or if he was just unlucky enough to be in the wrong place at the wrong time. I do know that, while David was still living in The Bottom, he'd been off the streets for almost a year when it happened, working a legit job as a maintenance man at a restaurant, doing everything he could to be there for his three kids, India, Nashon, and Aubrey, and still hoping to find a way out for them all.

—

Because of the coronavirus, we held the service graveside. My whole family was there, holding each other up and surrounding my mother with whatever strength we could spare. It was gray and rainy and cold. Folks were already being warned to stay home and away from large gatherings, but despite all that, more than three hundred people came to say goodbye to my big brother. From their stories and tears, it quickly became apparent to me that he'd had a personal relationship with almost all of them. David was no saint, but the people who were there that day didn't see him as a criminal or an ex-con; they saw his big heart and his generous soul. Folks talked about how well respected he'd been in our neighborhood, how selfless he was, what a good friend he'd been to them. If he thought a kid was hungry, he'd take them into a *papi* store, buy them something to eat, and then walk them back home and make sure they got there safe. If someone needed help fixing anything in their home, he was always happy to lend a hand. Dozens of people took me aside and told me how he never stopped talking about how proud he was of me and Gerb.

—

Losing my brother felt like both my worst nightmare come true, and deeply inevitable. I had been lying awake night after night, staring at the ceiling, preparing myself for this loss, for years. No matter what I accomplished or how far away from The Bottom I managed to get, at the end of the day I still waited for the phone to ring. The only question would be which name I'd hear when the bad news finally came. I'd done everything I was supposed to do. I'd won the championship, earned the college degree and the well-paying job, moved into the high-rise apartment that kept me safe and tucked away twenty-four stories up over the city. But no matter what I did or how much I distanced myself, The Bottom could still yank me back into its grasp and shatter my heart with its senseless violence.

—

Some might try to say that David got what he deserved. He used to deal, he went to prison, he left the barn. He never played it safe. But David was as precious as anyone in this story. He was a father and a brother and a son. He was a man with dreams and plans. He was just trying to survive. He hoped for more.

He loved and he was loved.

—

I spoke at the funeral. I told the story of how, when I was a little kid, I wanted nothing so much as I wanted to tag along after David and Bee, follow them wherever they were going, but David always insisted that I stay home.

He thought I was a pain in the ass, I said, laughing. *A little pest who was too slow and scared to be worth taking anywhere.*

I'd always thought about it that way, from the point of view of the child I had been. I thought that my brother just couldn't be bothered with me, that he was simply refusing to give me something I wanted. But then I started to think about what he did give me, and I realized I had been seeing it all wrong.

David could have let me follow him into trouble. Lots of big brothers in our neighborhood let their little brothers do just that. They used the younger kids as lookouts and witnesses and errand boys. They didn't take the time to argue or push them back into the house. They shrugged their shoulders and led them out into the life.

But David didn't do that.

He insisted I stay home. He left me behind where it was safer. He didn't allow me to follow him into streets.

As I stood there in the rain, beside his open grave, it finally hit me that maybe my brother hadn't just been pushing me away; maybe he'd also been doing his best to keep me safe. Maybe his reasons for keeping me at home had been more about protection than rejection.

Because the one time David did agree to take me with him, he led me to the barn.

Maybe he didn't realize it then, but David saved my life. He brought me to the horses, he showed me a world I never knew existed. He was the first person to lift me onto a pony. The first person to lead me around the ring. He opened the door that changed everything for me. He handed me the map that led me out of the same streets that would take his life so many years later.

When it came to his own safety, David had always been fearless, reckless even. But when it came to me, his little brother, he didn't let me take a single chance. He delivered me to the best, safest place he could find, and then, as always, he slipped away.

APPENDIX

THE RULES OF POLO

There are two types of polo: field and arena. Throughout the book, we mainly play arena polo, so the following rules apply to that version of the game.

The earliest version of polo was believed to have been played by nomads in Persia around 250 BCE. It quickly became a game played almost exclusively by nobility. By the Middle Ages it had spread throughout much of the world and was often used to train cavalry. The version of polo that we play in modern times originated in the royal courts of India in the early 1600s.

In arena polo, there are three players and the game is played indoors on dirt or sand. The arena is enclosed and measures 300 by 150 feet. There are two goal posts on either end of the arena. There are four seven-and-a-half-minute chukkers (the periods into which a game is divided) per twenty-eight-minute game. Players change out their ponies between each chukker, though some ponies may play more than one chukker after a rest.

The season for arena polo is late fall through early spring.

The players are all mounted on polo ponies. Polo ponies are actually highly trained horses, but are called "ponies" because traditionally, the game was played on smaller-sized horses. This is no longer true, but the horses are still trained to be as fast and agile as a pony.

The designated positions on each team are numbered one through three. Player number one is primarily offensive, player number two is offense/defense (equivalent to a soccer midfielder), and player number three is generally the most skilled and experienced player and the captain of the team. All team members are expected to be flexible enough to switch to any position if needed within a game. All the players are allowed to score goals.

Each player is given a handicap from negative two (the least skilled) to ten. Only a small number of the world's professional players are awarded a ten-goal handicap.

The game starts with a bowl-in. The players line up in the center of the arena on their respective sides, and one of two mounted umpires bowls the ball into the arena. The teams then compete for control of the ball.

The players use a long, rattan cane mallet to hit the ball, and they must stay within "the line of the ball," an imaginary line that extends through the ball along the line of travel. This line is set for the safety of both the players and the ponies. A player may approach the line from either side, but crossing this line will result in a penalty.

A player may execute a "rideoff"—meaning they make

shoulder-to-shoulder contact with another player's horse to throw them off the line—and take possession of the ball. They may also "hook" the other player's mallet in order to block a hit or a goal.

Players make a goal when they hit the ball between the goal posts. A pony can also make a goal for the team. After each goal, the players change directions. The team with the most goals at the end of the last chukker is declared the winner.

ACKNOWLEDGMENTS

As a young boy from The Bottom, never did I imagine writing a memoir at the age of twenty-seven. This book was possible because of countless people who opened doors and gave me a second chance at life. My debt and gratitude are boundless.

Nacho Figueras, thank you for introducing me to Emma and encouraging me to write this memoir. From afar, you have always believed in me and saw the importance of telling my story. Not only are you a great ambassador for the sport of polo, but your work off the field inspires me.

To the staff and faculty at Valley Forge Military Academy and College, thank you for taking a fragile boy from Philadelphia and preparing me for the world outside of academics and sports.

Thank you, Mr. Dan Crawford, for all your support. You are one of many people who put me in a position to succeed.

To my family, friends, staff, board members, and volunteers

from the Work to Ride program, thank you. Together you all saved the lives of many vulnerable kids.

Colorado State University, thank you. To my fellow Ram teammates, you made my four years in Fort Collins special. Together we studied, partied, and won a national championship. Andrew Wildermuth, Jered Berg, Alex Kokesh, Scott Cunningham, and James Dodge will always have a special place in my heart. Also, my roommate Jacob Kimiecik, and my dearest friend Nyle Tewahade.

To all my work colleagues, thank you for always believing in me and supporting my efforts outside the office. Joe and Frank Manheim, you two inspire me every day to become a better leader and businessman. I will forever be grateful for the opportunity you gave me.

To my Work to Ride teammates and fellow barn rats: Together we learned how to groom a horse, muck a stall, ride a horse, and swing a polo mallet. More importantly, we became a family away from our homes. You all inspired me to write this memoir. Whenever I was facing adversity, I could turn to my Work to Ride family. Thank you, Kevin Jones, Drea Taylor, Richard Prather, Tasha Harris, Brandon Rease, John Fields, Chris Perren, Lonnie Fields, Shadaria Shuler, Shariah Harris, Sharee Harris, Marc Harris.

The entire team at St. Martin's Press was incredibly enthusiastic and supportive throughout the development of the book. Thank you to my editor, Sara Goodman, for your guidance and helping me deliver my story to the world.

I want to thank my literary agent, Emma Parry, for shepherding this project from its inception. Your tenacious efforts made this possible. I appreciate you guiding me through this journey. Thank you, E.

Maia Rossini, thank you for helping me develop this book. I am beyond grateful to have met and worked with you. You are incredibly talented, and I cannot thank you enough.

I'm indebted to my entire family: my three brothers, David, Jabarr, and Daymar; two sisters, Kareema and Washika; and my mother, Lazette. Together we faced unimaginable issues but remained united. You allowed me to tell our story and share some of the darkest times. Thank you. Without you all, there would be no me. I am incredibly blessed to have you as a mother, Lazette. And grateful to have you all as my siblings.

Lastly, to the woman who sacrificed her life to save mine and many others, thank you, Lezlie Hiner. For more than two decades, you have opened doors and broken barriers. You turned my dreams into reality. I have a story to tell because of you.

This book is dedicated to all victims of gun violence,
my late brother David Rosser,
and my dearest friend, Mecca Harris.